LOST DEPARTMENT STORES
of
SAN FRANCISCO

LOST DEPARTMENT STORES

of

SAN FRANCISCO

Anne Evers Hitz

Foreword by Leah Garchik
Former Columnist, *San Francisco Chronicle*

THE
History
PRESS

Published by The History Press
Charleston, SC
www.historypress.com

Copyright © 2020 by Anne Evers Hitz
All rights reserved

Front cover, top, left to right: OpenSFHistory/wnp27.6429.jpg; Library
of Congress, HABS CAL,38-SANFRA,135--24; Fred Lyon; *bottom*:
OpenSFHistory/wnp25.4639.jpg.
Back cover, top: San Francisco History Center, San Francisco Public Library;
bottom: OpenSFHistory/wnp100.00065.jpg.

First published 2020

Manufactured in the United States

ISBN 9781467140713

Library of Congress Control Number: 2019954255

Dedicated to my great-great-grandfather F.W. Dohrmann and the generations who came before us. Thanks to those stalwart, innovative immigrants who made their way to the West Coast and focused their considerable energies into creating a magical city known as "the city that knows how" (with thanks to President William Howard Taft and Herb Caen). I'm honored to get to tell some of your stories.

CONTENTS

FOREWORD

When you grow up in a city, it's likely that by the time you go downtown with a few dollars to spend, you patronize the store where your mother took you to see the Christmas tree, where she took you to buy your first bra. You know where it's deluxe, you know where it's economical. And, even more complicated, you're familiar with all the terrain in between.

Coming to town as an adult, however, the shopping landscape is foreign. What's more, deciding where to best find the silks, satins and denims that will serve as self-expression has to be preceded by figuring out what the self, or the wannabe self, is.

Hippie in flowing florals? Social swan in almost-Chanel? Working woman in tailored suit?

It was no small task to find just the right store. Coming to San Francisco in the early '70s, it took months/years studying newspaper ads for the variety of stores I hadn't known back east—the White House, I. Magnin, J. Magnin, Ransohoff's, City of Paris—to decide where I was likely to find the best half-slip (remember those?), the best handbag, the best hip-huggers and (to me in particular) the best sales.

Every one of the stores mentioned above is gone now, so all of my acquired knowledge about these choices is of little use. (If only brain cells had a delete button.) Still, my memory bank includes snapshots of both the main floors of those stores, accessories illuminated by radiant skylights, and the shadowy corners of those stores, where racks of off-beat merchandise on sale awaited the bargain-hunters.

FOREWORD

We arrived in San Francisco just after the era when ladies who lunched wore gloves and hats to stroll through Union Square and just past the era when bare-breasted maidens swayed to rock-and-roll in the Panhandle. What to wear and where to buy it—and what did that teach us about the city? Anne Evers Hitz tells us the stories behind the stores.

—Leah Garchik,
former columnist, *San Francisco Chronicle*

PREFACE

As a fifth-generation San Franciscan, I grew up being told stories about "old" San Francisco. I would hear that some ancestor of mine (F.W. Dohrmann, my great-great-grandfather) had been involved in the Emporium, but as a typical kid, I really didn't pay much attention. It wasn't until I was an adult and became more interested in local history that it really piqued my interest. When I first began work on my book on the Emporium department store (Arcadia, 2014), I met many other natives with tales to tell about growing up in the city. Whether one grew up in the Sunset, Mission, Richmond, Noe Valley, Presidio Heights or Pacific Heights, you all had memories of going downtown as a kid.

I also encountered many former Emporium employees, and I was struck by how much they enjoyed working there (most of them!) and how the experience affected their lives. Hearing those stories and the nostalgia for the old stores and downtown experiences prompted me to consider researching and writing about six of the grand old stores and their beginnings and legacies. I am sure there will be those who say, "But why not Roos Brothers, Livingston's, Ransohoff's or O'Connor, Moffatt & Co.?" Time and resources were factors, of course, but also telling the stories of these six stores alone filled a volume. Enjoy.

ACKNOWLEDGEMENTS

So many people have helped me along the way. Kudos to my husband, who listened to my endless tales of San Francisco retail nostalgia. The patient librarians, historians, photo archivists and photographers who helped me and answered my many questions deserve thanks as well: Christina Moretta and Jeff Thomas, San Francisco History Center, San Francisco Public Library; Katy Guyon, San Francisco Municipal Transportation Agency (SFMTA) Photography Department and Archive; Patricia Keats, Society of California Pioneers; California State Library; David Gallagher, OpenSFHistory.org; and the Bancroft Library.

Thanks to my friends at San Francisco City Guides for their encouragement and to these individuals who shared their experiences or helped me in some way: Linda Ach, Nancy Bacall, Sandy Barbour, Richard Bayne, Bruce Bennett, Cathy Cooke, Arthur Corbin, Frank Dunnigan, Lolly Erlanger, Gloria Frere, Leah Garchik, Margaret Gault, Sally Gerstein, Bernadette Hooper, Andrew Howard, Barbara Koeth, Fred Lyon, Brent McDaneld, Ginnie Miraglia, Ellen Magnin Newman, Richard Parker, Therese Polletti, Ron Ross, Carole Cosgrove Terry, Carol Walker and Denise Pereira Webster. I'm also grateful to the Institute for Historical Study for supporting my research with a mini-grant. And let's not forget the many Facebook members who love to weigh in about growing up in San Francisco.

I would also like to gratefully acknowledge the permission granted to reproduce the copyrighted material in this book. Every effort has been made to trace copyright holders and to obtain their permission for the use of copyrighted material. I apologize for any errors or omissions and would be grateful if notified of any corrections that should be incorporated into future reprints or editions of this book.

INTRODUCTION

In the middle part of the last century, "going downtown" in San Francisco was a treat. You *always* got dressed up—hats and gloves for your mother and grandmother and good clothes for you (dresses and patent leather Mary Jane shoes for the girls, of course). Blue jeans weren't even a remote possibility.

Off you went for a day of shopping and eating around Union Square and Market Street, whether it was a visit to the Emporium to see Santa and the rooftop carnival at Christmas or stopping for Coffee Crunch Cake at Blum's or creamed spinach at Townsend's. Well-coiffed ladies who wanted to see and be seen attended the Monday Lunches in the Mural Room at the St. Francis Hotel, where they hoped Ernest, the headwaiter and majordomo, would seat them at the best tables.

Luxury department stores, many established in the last half of the nineteenth century, lined Union Square, their classy façades hinting at all the treasures to be had inside. City of Paris, with its seventy-foot Eiffel Tower on the roof, and I. Magnin, the "marble lady," were on Geary Boulevard at Stockton Street, facing Union Square. The St. Francis Hotel loomed on the west side of the square on Powell Street, the Powell/Hyde cable car clanking along the street in front. The massive White House store was a block from Union Square on Grant and Sutter, while Gump's resided at 250 Post Street for over eighty-five years. Young upstart Joseph Magnin, founded in 1913, was on Stockton Street, just south of the main square. Although the Emporium was located a couple of blocks away on the south side of

Looking southeast at Union Square from Post and Powell Streets at I. Magnin, Macy's, Blum's and Dohrmann's lined up along Geary Boulevard. *OpenSFHistory/wnp14.10052.jpg.*

Market Street (which didn't have the prestige of Union Square because it was considered more of a working-class area), it still had a loyal clientele. Other old retail establishments that locals remember fondly that are no longer part of the San Francisco retail landscape include Roos Brothers, Livingston's, Hale's, Ransohoff's, H. Liebes, Podesta Baldocchi, O'Connor, Moffatt & Co., Butler Bros., Weinstein's and Hastings.

Frank Dunnigan, author of *Growing Up in San Francisco's Western Neighborhoods*, shared with me his memories of "going downtown" during the holidays, which will strike a chord with those lucky enough to have grown up in San Francisco:

> *Our family's holiday shopping in the late 1950s and early 1960s always began with a ride on the L-Taraval streetcar. Through the Twin Peaks tunnel we would go, and by the time we reached downtown, the car was packed. As it slid past Fifth Street and stopped in front of the Emporium, it seemed that most of the passengers disembarked all at once.*

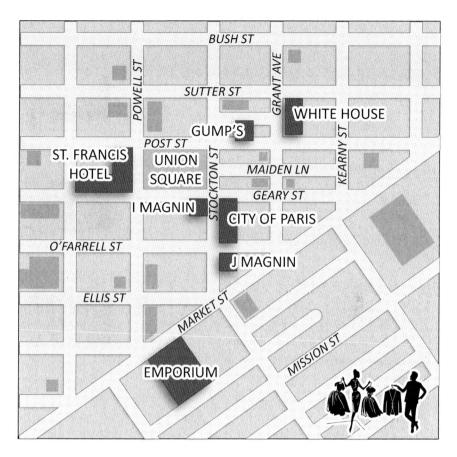

Union Square was at the center of the major shopping streets. The stores clustered nearby, except for the Emporium, which was south of Market Street. *Author's collection.*

Through the crowded main aisle we would go, as Mom and Grandma made a few purchases from the Notions Department before taking the back elevators up to the enormous Toy Department on the fourth floor. Mom would do her shopping there, as Grandma took the kids to see Santa and roof rides. From there, we would cross Market Street for lunch at Woolworth's and a bit more shopping—often candy, candles and other holiday items—and then on to see the tree at City of Paris. While Mom and Grandma shopped for clothing and gifts, kids insisted on viewing the thousands of ornaments and twinkling lights up close from the balconies on each floor.

We then walked up to Grant Avenue to see and smell the lavish floral and fir decorations at Podesta Baldocchi, ooh-ing and ah-ing at the windows

Clowning for a photographer at Union Square, looking southeast to the City of Paris, 1930s. *OpenSFHistory/wnp27.0620.jpg.*

at Gump's, and then a bit more shopping at the White House. Walking back to Union Square, there would be a stop in the Cosmetics Department at I. Magnin, while the ladies might pay a visit to the store's lavish lounge. If the kids were especially well-behaved, there might be a sweet treat from Blum's right next door before heading home.

Often, if we were carrying a lot of packages, Mom would call Dad at home and ask him to drive down and meet us. We then returned to the Emporium where Dad would be pulling up at the store's rear entrance on the Jessie Street alley. Clambering down to the bottom of Emporium's rear stairway, we would pile into the car with our shopping bags and head home, tired but happy—and all ready for the holidays.[1]

Although the memories linger, all these stores are now gone. Gump's, however, has a new owner and has announced the opening of a temporary "pop-up" store during the 2019 holiday season. Of the major ones (the ones

Podesta Baldocchi, on Grant Avenue between Sutter and Post Streets, always had fabulous window displays, which made for a not-to-be-missed experience on a trip downtown. *OpenSFHistory/wnp27.5625.jpg.*

Above: Looking south on Geary Boulevard in the 1950s, with Townsend's mid-block and Morrow's Nut House. *OpenSFHistory/ wnp100.00094.jpg.*

Left: Who could resist Blum's iconic Coffee Crunch Cake or Coffee Toffee Pie? The perfect end to a downtown excursion. *Author's collection.*

A flower stand at Post Street near Stockton in the 1930s. *OpenSFHistory/wnp37.01748.jpg*

covered in this book), the White House was the first to close, in 1965, and Gump's was the last, closing its doors in 2018. A Philip Johnson–designed modern building houses Neiman Marcus where the Beaux-Arts City of Paris building used to be. A developer bought I. Magnin's regal white building, which was a Macy's until early 2019. Part of the old White House is a parking garage. Saks Fifth Avenue, Apple, Tiffany, Macy's, Bulgari, Louis Vuitton and Williams-Sonoma storefronts line the square. Of these, only Williams-Sonoma, founded by Chuck Williams in 1956 in Sonoma and relocating in 1958 to San Francisco, is what we might consider "local."

BOOTS ON THE GROUND

The immigrants who founded some of the old stores came to San Francisco with thousands of others in search of a better life. Their descendants, schooled in the intricacies of catering to San Francisco clientele, carried on the tradition. When I spoke with Ellen Magnin Newman, one of the creative minds behind Joseph Magnin and a great-granddaughter of Mary Ann Magnin, founder of I. Magnin, she emphasized how important it was to have the owner present: "The best fertilizer is the foot of the owner on the soil. In every store the owner was present."

Abraham L. "A.L." Gump, wearing his trademark red carnation in his lapel, greeted Gump's customers in the store. Paul Verdier, of the City of Paris, had a private dining room for guests located behind the Cellars in the store's famed Normandy Lane. Mary Ann Magnin still visited the San Francisco flagship I. Magnin store often, even after she retired. (She lived in an apartment at the St. Francis Hotel, a half block away, so it was not much of a trek.) Ellen Magnin Newman's father, Cyril Magnin, whose creative vision built Joseph Magnin into a fashion powerhouse for youthful women on the West Coast, loved San Francisco and could be seen everywhere, from the flagship store's selling floor to the opera and official receptions (in his role as San Francisco's chief of protocol) to performances of *Beach Blanket Babylon*. He also walked to work every day from his apartment at the Mark Hopkins Hotel, while his driver would give his dog a ride in the car.

Let's take a look back at San Francisco's early days when opportunities abounded for enterprising newcomers.

FAST GROWTH AND OPPORTUNITIES

On the West Coast, the last half of the nineteenth century saw explosive growth in the population of San Francisco. After word got out about the discovery of gold in 1848, an estimated 300,000 people came to California seeking fortunes. The population in San Francisco increased exponentially, from fewer than 400 in 1847 to almost 30,000 residents by the end of 1849. This rapid influx of people inspired this 1849 note in the *Alta California* newspaper:

> *FASHIONABLE INDICATIONS—We shall soon have need of tailors, dress makers and milliners in our good city. Young gentlemen are "coming out" with their stand up collars, spring-gaiter pants and extensive displays of broad cloth, while the few ladies we have in town are not behind in the spreading of silks and satins. We shall soon have an "upper ten thousand" and an Opera House, but in the meantime we would advise young gentlemen*

not to swell too much for fear of a collapse or explosion. The over-dressed man is looked upon as either a fop or a fool, and is probably both.[2]

It was a city of immigrants. People born in Ireland, Germany, China and Italy accounted for one of every three San Francisco residents by the end of the 1860s, when the city's population numbered more than 100,000. In 1890, the population approached 300,000.[3] Although the gold and silver booms had wound down by 1890, there was new money in town, and the city's red-light district, the Barbary Coast, was in full swing. San Francisco had an air of prosperity and was a cosmopolitan metropolis with a frontier edge. All those new residents, many with new fortunes, had money to spend and needed goods for establishing households and required tailors, hatters, dress and shirt makers, jewelers and other merchants for sartorial elegance. As an 1893 editorial about San Francisco's millionaires in the *Argonaut* pointed out:

> *San Francisco has a long list of abnormally rich men. There are more millionaire fortunes in San Francisco than in any other American city, and, we presume, more than in any European city of corresponding population, unless it may be Amsterdam or Frankfort. It is a curious fact, and without one exception, that none spring from the wealthy class, nearly everyone from the very poorest class, and that only one brought any money to San Francisco....From poor men to rich men, they have grown up among us, and, with the exception of the exceptional few—and they the ones of lowest education, of the most obscure birth, and of blemished reputations, who have gone abroad—conduct themselves with as much sense and modesty as though they were not rich.*[4]

GRAND EMPORIUMS TAKE CENTER STAGE

At the end of the nineteenth century, grand emporiums dominated the retail landscape in cities across the United States, and San Francisco was no different. It was an era when the big stores and great merchants marched forward, eclipsing the dry goods and general stores. By the end of the century, there were American department stores across the country, many housed in beautiful buildings, with hundreds of thousands of shoppers a day coming through their doors. Window shopping became a leisure activity.

What made a great department store? In the era before the automobile, a central location serviced by mass transportation was an imperative. The successful store often had a very visible owner who built relationships with the community and employees. The store offered a great variety of goods to entice customers into the store, prices were lower and it offered free services such as deliveries, liberal credit arrangements and merchandise-return privileges. The store was strictly departmentalized, appealed to the masses and was a big advertiser. Salespeople provided individual attention, and there was a feeling of trust between seller and buyer and between employer and employee. Employees often worked at the same store for their entire careers. It was an era when many women did not work outside the home and could enjoy a daylong shopping trip with afternoon tea and a concert.

SHOPPING DISTRICT EVOLVES

For the first few decades after 1850, the fashionable shopping district in San Francisco was along Market, Kearny and Stockton Streets, east of the area that would become Union Square. Journalist Will Irwin describes the lively social scene, reminiscent of the Spanish leisurely stroll, or *paseo*:

> *The greatest beauty-show on the continent was the Saturday afternoon matinee parade in San Francisco....It belonged to the middle class....From two o'clock to half-past five, a solid procession of Dianas, Hebes and Junos passed and repassed along the five blocks between Market and Powell and Sutter and Kearney [sic]—the "line" of San Francisco slang. Along the open-front cigar stores, characteristic of the town, gilded youth of the cocktail route gathered in knots to watch them.*[5]

In 1850, John W. Geary, the first mayor of San Francisco, deeded to the city the public square that would become Union Square, a tall sand dune at the time. He stipulated that it be held in perpetuity as a park. Soon, the sand dunes were gone and many of the lots surrounding the square sold for residences. During the Civil War, people gathered for pro-Union rallies in the square, and it became Union Square.

During the 1880s, the square became the center of a fashionable residential district, with a few churches scattered about. By the turn of the century, offices and stores dominated. The Spring Valley Water Co. owned

The Dewey Monument in Union Square (1918), decorated with patriotic bunting, with a sign urging people to buy Liberty Bonds. *California History Room, California State Library, Sacramento, California.*

the southeast corner of Geary and Stockton Streets, the future home of the City of Paris. Real estate speculator C.C. Butler (who built the first Cliff House at the western edge of the city in 1863) was building the Butler Building on the southwest corner of Geary Boulevard and Stockton Street (the future home of I. Magnin).

The years 1903 and 1904 were key in the square's evolution. Thousands of San Franciscans turned out in 1903 to greet President Theodore Roosevelt, who came to San Francisco to dedicate the Dewey monument in a newly designed Union Square. The seventy-nine-foot monument, topped by its bronze "Winged Victory," commemorated Commodore George Dewey's victory at the Battle of Manila Bay in the Philippines. The opening of the world-class St. Francis Hotel on the west side of the square in March 1904 was the crowning glory for the area and went a long way toward establishing San Francisco as the "Paris of the West."

ST. FRANCIS HOTEL: A STUNNING ADDITION

On opening night, a line of carriages and automobiles three blocks long containing the cream of San Francisco politicians, businessmen and society approached the grand hotel. In the breathless prose of a *San Francisco Chronicle* reporter:

> *The assemblage was brilliant in the extreme and fit for the richness of the settings and the beauty of the floral decorations....The Hotel St. Francis has come into the social life of San Francisco in a blaze of glory surpassing the most roseate expectations of those who were looking forward to the opening of the stately new graystone edifice looming up twelve stories high and commanding a magnificent frontal outlook over beautiful, lawn-capped Union square, right in the heart of the city.*[6]

Once guests paraded up past the granite pillars to the lobby, they found a lounge, a four-thousand-volume library and a basement grill decorated with beer steins, elk horns and the head of an Alaskan moose. The 450 guest rooms had private baths, telephones and steam heat. Designed by Walter Bliss and William Faville, the hotel was commissioned by the trustees of the estate of Charles Crocker, one of the founders of the Central Pacific Railroad, for the benefit of Crocker's three young grandchildren.

Above: In 1919, a grand vision: the St. Francis Hotel and Union Square sparkling at night. *California History Room, California State Library, Sacramento, California.*

Right: For Monday Lunch at the St. Francis Hotel's Mural Room, one dressed to impress not only the other attendees but also Ernest, the headwaiter who ruled the room, seating the chosen few at the best tables. *St. Francis Hotel.*

FIRE DECIMATES THE SHOPPING DISTRICT

Of course, everything changed after April 18, 1906, as the fire raged for days after the great earthquake. Newspapers all over the country carried the story of the earthquake and devastating fire that threatened to destroy the entire city. Buildings around the square, including the St. Francis, were either completely destroyed or gutted. Union Square became the site of the Mrs. W.H. Crocker camp, one of the army's twenty-one refugee camps for the quake victims.

Many of the department stores set up temporary headquarters on Van Ness Avenue. The city set about rebuilding, and the Union Square area became even more of a retail center. The Emporium reopened in late 1908. The City of Paris's luxurious new Beaux-Arts building opened in March 1909. Gump's opened at 250 Post Street in 1909 as well. Little by little, San Francisco was back in business.

Refugees from the 1906 earthquake and fire at the Mrs. William H. Crocker relief camp, Union Square. *California History Room, California State Library, Sacramento, California.*

THE ERA OF THE AUTOMOBILE

Parking became a big problem. More and more people could afford cars, and of course, they wanted to drive downtown to one of the many hotels, large retail stores, office buildings, clubs and theaters, but the capacity of nearby garages was very limited. By the 1940s, congested streets surrounding Union Square became such an issue that the city hired

Top: View of Union Square looking north around 1940, with the St. Francis Hotel on Powell Street at the left. *California History Room, California State Library, Sacramento, California.*

Bottom: Constructing the underground garage beneath Union Square in early 1940s. It could also be used as an air raid shelter. *California History Room, California State Library, Sacramento, California.*

Union Square in 1960 during a Nixon rally, viewed from the St. Francis Hotel, with the City of Paris and I. Magnin at right. *OpenSFHistory/wnp14.3767.jpg.*

architect Timothy Pflueger (who would also design the future I. Magnin building) to design a garage serving the Union Square area. In March 1941, they broke ground for a 1,700-car, four-level garage under the square. Despite it being wartime, the Union Square garage was finished by the summer of 1942. It was only because of its potential alternate use as a bomb shelter or as an emergency hospital that special materials were released for the garage's completion.

FAST-FORWARD

Mid-century onward, the shopping area continued to evolve. One by one, the old stores discussed in this book closed, to be replaced by stores such as Neiman Marcus, Tiffany & Co. and Saks Fifth Avenue that had their roots elsewhere. Nordstrom and Bloomingdale's anchor the nearby Westfield

A 1979 aerial view of Union Square from the St. Francis Hotel; I. Magnin, the "marble lady," is on the right. *California History Room, California State Library, Sacramento, California.*

San Francisco Centre, former home of the Emporium. International boutiques, national specialty stores and jewelry stores moved in. The city struggled to keep the shopping district attractive to locals and tourists as pigeons, vagrants and even rats became a problem. The creation of the Union Square Business Improvement District in 1999 and a renovation in 2002 helped improve the area, but the city continues to deal with a seemingly intractable homeless problem.

"Going downtown" these days does not have the lure that it once had. Parking is expensive, public transportation crowded and why go downtown if Amazon has everything anyway? The stores are making efforts to add services to compete. If you buy something at Macy's online and it's in stock at the downtown store, you can pull up to the curb on O'Farrell Street and a Macy's employee will bring it to your car. The stores are also pushing for same-day delivery to your home to compete with the online world. Personal shoppers abound. But the retail landscape is cutthroat as the stores try to compete with the Internet and shifting shopping habits. It makes one long for a time when you could spend a leisurely day downtown shopping with a friend, being greeted by proprietor Raphael Weill as you had tea in the White House tearoom and going to hear a concert at the Emporium. As San Francisco's own Herb Caen, who was the unofficial chronicler of the city's bygone days, once wrote:

> *Not all that long ago you could've walked into Bank of America on Montgomery and shaken hands with A.P. Giannini. Yes, A.P. in person, sitting at a desk in the middle of the main floor. Grover Magnin would show you around his beloved I. Magnin store—"the most beautiful in the world," and he meant it—and Cyril Magnin was delighted to wait on you at J. Magnin. "I. or J., Magnin's the way," beamed Cyril.…There were live Gumps at Gump's, Prentis Hale at Hale Bros., Michel Weill at the White House (founded by his uncle) and Paul Verdier parading his poodle at the City of Paris or buying you a champagne in Normandie [sic] Lane. Come on along, come on along and buy a blazer from Bobby Roos at Roos Bros., a sweater from Carl Livingston at Livingston's, a dress from one of the many Liebeses at H. Liebes.[7]*

Let's take a look back at these early San Francisco retail institutions and the innovative, colorful, hardworking powerhouses who built them.

Chapter 1

CITY OF PARIS, 1850–1972

"It May Rock but Never Sinks"

Imagine the chaotic scene on the San Francisco waterfront in 1850. News of the 1848 gold discovery had reached far shores, and thousands were traveling to California to seek their fortunes, many by boat. Since this was almost twenty years before the completion of the first Transcontinental Railroad, the options for getting to California were via boat around Cape Horn, via the Isthmus of Panama or overland.

The waterfront was crowded with ships, and it was difficult to find a place to berth. The city's narrow streets and harbor were overflowing with people, ships and wagons. There were many ships on the bay that had been abandoned, deserted by their crews so that they could rush to the gold fields as soon as the ships cast anchor. Passengers on ships, after a long, arduous journey—whether they had sailed around Cape Horn (four to eight months) or crossed the Isthmus of Panama (two to three months)—often had to wait for days before unloading.

In the spring of 1850, word got out that *La Ville de Paris* (City of Paris), a chartered three-mast schooner, had arrived laden with fine laces, wines, Cognac and Champagne. Two entrepreneurial Frenchmen, brothers Emile and Félix Verdier, were responsible for the boat and its precious cargo. Félix had procured all the goods in France and sent his brother to California to sell the luxury products that only France could provide.

Emile embarked at Le Havre and landed in Colón, Panama, where he crossed the Isthmus of Panama with the valuable merchandise loaded on mules. Once he reached the Pacific coast, he chartered the *Ville de Paris* and

The store's seventy-foot replica of the Eiffel Tower graced the roof, with "City of Paris Since 1850" for all to see. *Library of Congress, HABS CAL,38-SANFRA,135--24.*

set sail for San Francisco. Floating from the mast was a flag with the motto "*Fluctuat nec mergitur*," roughly translated as "It may rock but never sinks," the Latin motto from the coat of arms of the city of Paris.

San Franciscans were so excited about the arrival of the high-quality cargo that they rowed out to the boat. "Before the 'Ville de Paris' had dropped anchor, small boats were alongside with gentlemen and their ladies, eager to see, touch and taste the wares aboard. A sampling bar was set up topside."[8] The cargo was all sold before it could be unloaded, and many patrons paid with gold dust. Emile Verdier headed back to France to procure more goods, and thus began the Ville de Paris (City of Paris) department store, which was to be in existence for another 122 years in San Francisco.

KEEPING IT IN THE FAMILY

Félix and Emile Verdier hailed from Nimes, France, where they ran a successful silk stocking business. The discovery of gold in California in January 1848 was just a month before a wave of riots in France. King Louis Philippe was overthrown in February 1848, and in December, Louis-Napoleon Bonaparte was elected president of the Second Republic. Three years later, Bonaparte suspended the elected assembly and became the emperor of France or Napoleon III. Supporters of the republic resented Napoleon III's harsh repressive actions against his opponents, and tens of thousands of Frenchmen got gold fever and set off to find their fortunes in California.

According to a City of Paris booklet published on the occasion of the store's seventy-fifth anniversary, it was Louise Adeline Verdier (Madame Verdier Fauvety), wife of Félix, who pushed for taking advantage of the golden opportunities in California and San Francisco. "While others are hunting for gold," she declared, "we will supply them with silken and lace finery for which they will spend their gold!"[9] Other merchants and manufacturers both in the United States and abroad had the same vision, but the lure of gold was too strong, and they hurried to the gold fields and abandoned their cargo. The Verdiers, on the other hand, opened their first store at 334 Clay Street between Montgomery and Kearny Streets, near Portsmouth Square, the center of the city's commercial section. By 1851, after a second trip to procure more goods, Emile had moved the store to larger quarters at 152 Kearny Street, the southeast corner of Sutter and Kearny.

Business took off after the move to Kearny Street, then the center of the city's shopping district. In 1854, Emile and Félix (who continued to live in Paris and take care of the purchases) established a partnership with Gustave and Antone Kaindler, who were novelty importers. The store, renamed Verdier and Kaindler, continued to expand and moved numerous times over the next few years.

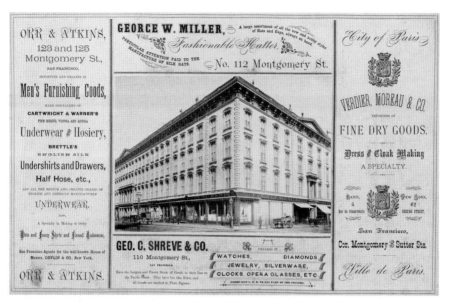

An 1880 ad features City of Paris, Verdier, Moreau & Co., located at fashionable Montgomery and Sutter Streets. *California History Room, California State Library, Sacramento, California.*

Emile died of yellow fever while on his third trip across the Isthmus of Panama in 1867, and Félix passed away in Paris in 1869. Madame Verdier Fauvety then sent her son, young Louis Gaston Verdier ("Gaston"), who was just twenty, to San Francisco to work with the Kaindlers as the store continued to grow.

Soon after Gaston's arrival, he helped direct the store's next move to the Occidental Hotel at the corner of Montgomery and Sutter Streets, where it would occupy the entire first floor. The new store opened on May 2, 1869.

FILLING A NEED

Imagine those miners, fresh from the gold fields, encountering the bonnets, Persian shawls, cotton and woolen stockings, petticoats, neck-handkerchiefs, laces and silks that the Verdiers offered. They wanted those beautiful goods for their wives or sweethearts, and the Verdiers had the resources to provide them with the latest fashions as well as baskets of Champagne, casks of rare wines and barrels of brandy (a tradition of selling fine vintages that the

Verdiers continued into the twentieth century with their Verdier Cellars). As described in the 1854 *Annals of San Francisco* (Frank Soule, ed.):

> *The presence of the French has had a marked influence upon society in San Francisco.…The expensive and fashionable style of dressing among the French ladies has greatly encouraged the splendid character of the shops of jewelers, silk merchants, milliners and others whom women chiefly patronize, while it has perhaps increased the general extravagance among the whole female population of the city.*[10]

With the flow of goods from Paris, San Franciscans were only one ship's voyage behind the latest Paris fashions. The French Argonauts (the name for those who moved to California during the gold rush) who stayed after the heady days of the gold rush ended built a vibrant French community with a hospital, newspaper, church and multiple social organizations. French capital helped build the city, and the French residents, including the Verdiers and other French businessmen such as Raphael Weill of the White House, contributed to the city's cosmopolitan culture, helping it earn the name "Paris of the Pacific."

In the 1850s, Paris and its stylish ladies were very influential on the fashions of the world and on San Francisco. According to "Sylvia," who wrote *Sylvia's*

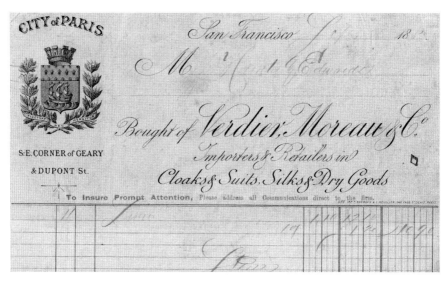

An invoice from Verdier, Moreau & Co.; in 1888, the store name changed to G. Verdier & Co. *CO54914. The Society of California Pioneers.*

Book of the Toilet: A Ladies Guide to Dress and Beauty in 1881, the French had a saying: "bien coiffé, bien gantée, bien chaussée," which translates to "well coiffed, well gloved, well shod"—something all ladies who wanted to emulate the French sense of style aspired to.[11] Author Julia Altrocchi, in *The Spectacular San Franciscans*, wrote:

> *It was in the early 1850s that that lovely lady of Paris, who was to have such a widespread (in every sense) influence upon the feminine fashions of the world, through crinolines, robes impératrices, Zouave jackets, bonnets and many other modes—the Empress Eugénie—first sent her designs rolling across the ocean. The hoop skirt or crinoline…was adopted by the French court in 1855 and, via the speediest clippers, reached the second Paris at the Golden Gate.*[12]

CONTINUING TO GROW

Soon after the store relocated to the Occidental Hotel, the Franco-Prussian War broke out, and Gaston Verdier embarked for France in 1870 to join the army to fight the Germans. Meanwhile, the store, still occupying the floor of the Occidental, changed its name from Verdier, Moreau & Co. to G. Verdier & Co. in 1888. Gaston was residing in Paris, and his partner, August Fusenot, managed the San Francisco store. It also moved a few more times and opened branches in Paris, New York and Los Angeles before moving into its final home on Union Square.

By 1896, Gaston had made his way back to San Francisco, this time with his sixteen-year-old son Paul. Gaston came to oversee another move of the store, this time to a building built by the Spring Valley Water Co. especially for the City of Paris. It was located at Geary and Stockton, one block west of the main shopping district on Kearny Street. Stockton Street was lined with wooden buildings and shacks on both sides.

The new store was on Union Square, which was not much more than a small park at the time, with a busy blacksmith across the street. The St. Francis Hotel was not to be built until many years later, in 1904. Although some doubted the commercial viability of such a location, Gaston's foresight was proven correct as the area was to become a center for luxury stores and the City of Paris occupied a key spot on the southeast corner, former site of the Wigwam theater.

THE DAY THE EARTH SHOOK

The City of Paris building's architect, Clinton Day, was very active in the Bay Area and designed several buildings on the University of California–Berkeley campus as well as the Gump's store on Post Street. Supposedly the first post-Victorian, Neoclassical structure on Union Square, the new City of Paris was to reside in a six-story, steel-frame Beaux-Arts commercial building. City of Paris occupied the bottom two floors, and the water company had the top four floors. City of Paris occupied this same spot until its closure in 1972.

The morning of April 18, 1906, twenty-four-year-old Paul Verdier, who had been appointed general manager of the store, was in his thirteenth-floor apartment at the St. Francis Hotel when he was rudely awakened by an armoire toppling over. As he recalled in his memoir:

> *I had only one thought: burglars. But it didn't take long before I realized that it was an earthquake....The noise was like the rush of wind through a forest with the difference that, instead of trees, it was steel beams that were groaning....I went immediately to the store which was a block from my hotel. The window mannequins had fallen face down as fallen soldiers and the wall of a neighboring building had smashed through a skylight. Besides this there was very little damage.*[13]

Little did Paul know of the conflagration that was to come. He and his father, Gaston, who was visiting from Paris, went to the store to move some of the more precious merchandise but were only able to save a fraction of the stock. They collected books, documents and important papers, plus $5,000 that was in the safe, and then went off to have lunch at Marchand's, the city's best French restaurant in those days. Paul said in his memoir that it was the last meal the restaurant served before flames consumed it. That evening, he headed back in his buggy in the direction of Union Square. The sky was black, and ashes were everywhere:

> *Crossing Van Ness Avenue, a half-burned piece of paper fell into my carriage. It was an invoice from the City of Paris which I recognized immediately by the letterhead with our motto: "Fluctuat nec mergitur." At the corner of Mason Street I was stopped by a police cordon. I explained that I was on my way to the store, the City of Paris, of which I was manager. "The City of Paris?—but it no longer exists! It burned down about an hour ago." There was no way to express my dismay.*[14]

43 Ruins of Marchand's Restaurant and City of Paris Dry Goods Co., after the fire of April 18 - 19 - 20, '06. San Francisco, Cal.

Top: The building was in a sad state after the 1906 fire. The interiors and most of the south and east walls were destroyed, while the two street façades survived. *Library of Congress, HABS CAL,38-SANFRA,135--72.*

Bottom: Looking southwest toward Union Square after the fire. Stockton Street and the City of Paris are on the left. *Library of Congress, LC-USZ62-64305.*

The interiors and most of the south and east walls of the building were destroyed, while the two street façades survived.

After the earthquake and fire, San Francisco residents and merchants got to work rebuilding their city and their lives. The City of Paris, along with some other leading merchants, set up a temporary store on Van Ness Avenue, which had not been affected by the fire. Within three weeks, the City of Paris had opened in the elegant Hobart mansion on Van Ness Avenue at Washington Street, while the store on Union Square was rebuilt.

In the Hobart mansion, they sold linens in the dining room, silks and laces in the drawing room, books in the library, "fluffy French lingerie"[15] in the bedrooms and wines in the wine cellar. Paul Verdier set up his office on the second floor. They were to be in this space for three years.

Meanwhile, by the end of November 1906, plans were filed for rebuilding the Stockton Street building, which the Spring Valley Water Co. sold to the Union Square Improvement Co. in 1908. City of Paris was to occupy the entire building.

For the rebuilding, the architect was Arthur Brown Jr. of Bakewell and Brown, whose other projects included San Francisco City Hall, the Opera House, Veterans Memorial at Civic Center and Coit Tower. A French architect, Louis Bourgeois, also aided in the design. All the architects trained at the School of Fine Arts (École des Beaux Arts) in Paris. Brown retained the pre-fire exterior but changed the interior so it would have a luxuriously detailed four-story, art glass–roofed rotunda. Its grand reopening was March 15, 1909.

STUNNING EXAMPLE OF LA BELLE ÉPOQUE

Martha Hutson, writing in *American Art Review* in the 1970s when the store was threatened with demolition, describes the elegant interior:

> *The visitor to the store passes from the light outdoors through the dark entrance way into an interior space of lightness and elegance. The store's floor space flows around a central four-story rotunda topped by an art glass skylight through which streams the sunlight. At each floor level below the skylight is a balcony that the visitor can approach to view the beauty of the rotunda both above and below. At the second- and third-story levels there are elaborate, delicately patterned iron railings. The color scheme is white and gold. Monumental columns surrounded by Corinthian capitals rise from the second level to the fourth floor up the sides of the rotunda.*[16]

Harry Ryle Hopps, who owned the United Glass Company with his brother Bert, designed the opalescent glass skylight. The design featured an image of the ship *La Ville de Paris* at full sail with the store's motto "*Fluctuat nec mergitur*" beneath. Set in a gold frame with elaborate carvings at each end, the elliptical fifty-five-by-thirty-six-foot skylight let light through in a blaze of belle-époque elegance. In addition to the skylight, a seventy-foot

Left: The epitome of belle-époque elegance, the elliptical fifty-five-by-thirty-six-foot skylight let light through to the center rotunda. *SFMTA Photo | SFMTA.com/photo.*

Below: A mythic, mustached face and cascading cornucopia support the concave art glass skylight. *Library of Congress, HABS CAL,38-SANFRA,135--62.*

replica of the Eiffel Tower graced the roof, with "City of Paris Since 1850" for all to see.

Following the First World War, when Paul Verdier became president, the store expanded into the D.N. & E. Walter Company building at the northeast corner of O'Farrell and Stockton Streets. Eventually, City of Paris had the full block on Stockton between O'Farrell and Geary. Branch stores opened in San Mateo, Stonestown, Vallejo and Marin-Northgate.

A SPECIAL STORE

City of Paris prided itself on its many specialty departments, which often represented a unique mix of France and San Francisco. Three of its most distinctive departments were Verdier Cellars, Normandy Lane and the Rotunda Gallery.

In describing Verdier Cellars, the store's marketing copy makes it sound as if the proprietors considered it their civic duty to sell good wine. In an undated company brochure,[17] store president Paul Verdier stated that they had the most complete wine cellar in America, offering more than one thousand varieties of vintage wines, select liqueurs and choice spirits. It was the first cellar to be opened after the repeal of Prohibition in 1933, "again signifying City of Paris' individuality and the unique service which San Franciscans have come to expect from us." Sounding like a manifesto, the brochure continues:

> **Why City of Paris Sells Wine**: *Because there is an opportunity to be of great service to our patrons in the sharing of our experience, we feel it is our duty to operate a wine and liquor department....We believe we can render a valuable service to our patrons and to California, because:*
>
> *First...the wines have been so badly abused during Prohibition that we want our customers to make use of our knowledge for guidance in their selection.*
>
> *Second...California, being the wine-producing state of America, we will help our own state in distributing the product of one of our principal industries directly from producer to consumer.*
>
> *Third...California was making very good wines before Prohibition and now with our close French connections, we can assist the producers to help make the very best wine in the world. Our advice to them would be to promote their wines under some typical California name.*

Fourth…We believe that wine on the table of California homes will prevent the return of Prohibition. But to insure this, good plain wines should be sold cheaply and within the reach of all American people.

Therefore, to "do our part," the City of Paris sells not only California wines but also the leading European wines.

Verdier moved quickly to get the first imported liquor stock in the United States after repeal. However, one of his first shiploads of liquor was put out on the docks in New York's cold weather because the ship had to sail again immediately.

The young Bordeaux wine aged ten years in one day. The old Bordeaux soured and couldn't take it. The champagne iced up and broke the bottles, but the Vermouth, a fortified wine, became a wonderful thing. Afterwards our customers commented on that wonderful Vermouth….We could not very well say, "Madame, it was frozen!"[18]

Emile Drevoir was the first manager of Verdier Cellars. He credited Paul Verdier's passion and knowledge about wine as the reason for its success. They had warehouses on the waterfront stocked with wines and liquors ready to bring to the store.

A Verdier Cellars ad from 1942 would make you weep. A bottle of Chateau Latour Haut Brion, 1925, or of Chateau Smith-Haut Lafitte, 1928, sold for $1.45; a case of either went for $16.50. Hundreds of wartime weddings were celebrated to the popping of French champagne corks at $4.95 a bottle…1921, 1922 and 1925 vintages.[19]

In the lower level, Verdier Cellars was part of the store's famed Normandy Lane. To get there, one entered a side door on O'Farrell Street or Geary Boulevard and went down some steps to what looked like a small street in Paris. It was like a stage set, with mismatched counters, uneven floors and drooping awnings. If you entered on the O'Farrell Street side, first you could stop at the French bookstore or the long stall with French magazines, dictionaries and novels. Or you could get your watch repaired at a shop across from the bookstore. If stamp collecting was your passion, there was a tiny booth that sold or exchanged rare stamps. Need a silhouette? Stop by Madame Kurtzweil's booth and she would work her magic scissors and make a black silhouette for you.

Right: *Mais oui*! An ad in French aimed at the French-speaking residents of California. *Kathleen Manning.*

Below: The store during its last days, before Neiman Marcus and its parent, Carter Hawley Hale, won the battle to tear it down for a new store. *Library of Congress, HABS CAL,38-SANFRA,135—1.*

After passing the cigarette and candy booth, if you were in search of "Tripe a la mode de Caen" (tripe stew, a traditional dish from Normandy cooked for five hours), served with spicy little cinnamon rolls, there was the popular Normandy Lane tearoom ready to serve you. Or perhaps you were in pursuit of some rotisserie chickens; Chef Victor Faure could make you happy. You could pick up some lovely almond macaroons or croissants at the patisserie as well.

At Verdier Cellars, why not stop and have a glass of wine at the Tchen-Tchen bar, whose counter was made from a striking red Chinoiserie lacquer bed? If you were a local politician, opera star or visiting dignitary, Paul Verdier might invite you into his private dining room with its circular table, located behind the Cellars.

ROTUNDA GALLERY

The fourth-floor rotunda became a gallery known for its high-quality exhibitions of ceramics, lithographs, watercolors, gouaches and art in other media. Displays were in the Rotunda Gallery and in the Little Gallery. Curator Beatrice Judd Ryan (known to all as "Mrs. Ryan") was a formidable art connoisseur who took over the art gallery at the City of Paris after serving as regional director for the state director of exhibitions of the Federal Arts Project during the Depression. During those difficult times, she had worked with many of the artists and muralists who painted at Coit Tower and the Beach Chalet. Known for her no-nonsense style, her colorful hats and always having violets in her hair, she helped keep artists gainfully employed during the challenging days of the '30s and then had her own gallery at 166 Geary and coordinated the "Art in Action" exhibition for the Golden Gate International Exposition at Treasure Island in 1939. Mrs. Ryan was the perfect curator to work with Paul Verdier and his sister, Madame Suzanne de Tessan, who also helped manage the store. Their goal was to attract the clientele who would be interested in local artists as well as art from artists such as Henri Matisse, Auguste Rodin, Toulouse Lautrec and Raoul Dufy. Exhibitions would change every few months, and opening receptions helped draw a crowd.

Eight pillars support the four-story oval rotunda, each with masks of women's faces wreathed with grape leaves and grape clusters. *Library of Congress, HABS CAL,38-SANFRA,135—78.*

MANY SPECIAL OFFERINGS

City of Paris offered clothing for the entire family. Individual "shops" included the Baby Shop, Girls' Shop, Boys' Shop, Co-Ed Shop, Deauville Sports Shop, Gown Salon, Coat and Suit Salons, Men's Store and Bridal Salon. Beyond the clothing for the family, there were special services such as stocking repair (a throwback to the years of the war when such luxuries were rare).

Gift seekers found what they were looking for in the City of Paris' Art Needlework and Tapestry room or the Gift Shop or the Pagoda Shop. At the Geary Boulevard entrance was the Perfume Bar, while at the Helena Rubinstein Make-up Vanity on the first floor, makeup artists were standing by to work their magic with a complimentary session. In the Beauty Salon Lounge was the Refreshment Bar, where women who were having their beauty needs attended to could have lunch or tea. Brentano's bookstore also offered a wide range of books.

Want a lamp shade with seventy yards of lace edging? The Mary Ann Paris Shop took care of requests like that, designing furniture and fabrics to fit the customers' needs. George de Bonis, who started in the store in 1914 as a stock boy and became president after Paul Verdier died, had a natural talent for interior decorating, and his knowledge of fine furnishings and antiques helped the store's home furnishings department become well known. Rooms for period furniture were paneled with the wood of the period, imported from France.

CHRISTMAS WONDERLAND

During the holidays, every kid in San Francisco wanted to kick off the season by visiting City of Paris to see its wondrous tree and then go to the rooftop carnival at the Emporium. That City of Paris tree appeared as if by magic on the Monday after Thanksgiving. At 9:30 a.m., when the doors opened, there was the four-story, thirty-five-foot tree, completely decorated, turning on its seven-foot platform.

The stately Douglas fir, crowned with a giant star, came from the Inyo National Forest or somewhere near the Russian River. Traffic would be stopped on Geary Boulevard as the tree was carried, wrapped tightly in burlap, into the store.

At Christmas, the four-story, thirty-five-foot Douglas fir tree, completely decorated, would appear as if by magic on the Monday after Thanksgiving. *Library of Congress, HABS CAL,38-SANFRA,135--79.*

What luxurious item could be in this beautiful City of Paris box? A bonnet? A Persian shawl? A petticoat? Or perhaps a gift from the Pagoda Shop. *Ron Ross.*

After hoisting it into place on its platform, the crew of twenty worked all Saturday and Sunday nights decorating it with over five thousand colored glass balls, eight hundred yards of silver tinsel and many, many packages of glittery silver threads, or "rain." Next came the doll buggies, red wagons, snowmen, drums, horns, candy canes, stars and snowballs, plus a Santa Claus or two on the branches. Finally, the popcorn ropes. Soft white fabric wrapped the base. After admiring the tree, off you'd go to Blum's for a sweet and then on to the Emporium to skate and see Santa (more on that later in the Emporium chapter).

SO WHAT HAPPENED?

City of Paris continued to do well after the Second World War, but other downtown stores were slowly disappearing, including the White House, O'Connor, Moffatt & Co. and Ransohoff's. The world of retailing changed in those years after the war as chain and discount stores and off-price outlets began to proliferate. Shopping habits changed as well, as more women entered the workforce and the downtown shopping experience lost its luster. Shoppers didn't value the unique merchandise, individual attention and special services that were the hallmark of a store like City of Paris.

Paul Verdier left his position as president in 1958 to become chairman of the board. He died in 1966, and George de Bonis became president. The

City of Paris proudly displayed its signature boat and founding date on everything from playing cards to boxes and bags. *Author's collection and Ron Ross.*

A businessman in the '50s in front of the City of Paris exchanges greetings with a flower vendor on Stockton Street. *OpenSFHistory/wnp25.1483.jpg*

store could not compete with the chains and changing demographics and began to fail. First, the branch stores closed. Then Liberty House took over the Stonestown store.

In January 1972, Paul L. Chauvin, vice president of the store and nephew of Paul Verdier, issued this proud and almost defiant letter announcing the end of City of Paris. Chauvin also promised to honor all obligations.

> *January 25, 1972*
> *A message to the many good customers, friends and business associates of City of Paris and to all of its devoted employees:*
>
> *The descendants of Felix Verdier, the founder of City of Paris, sadly announce that after 122 years of catering to the good tastes and elegant requirements of many generations of San Franciscans, City of Paris will close its doors in the early spring of 1972.*
>
> *The time has now come when this Verdier-Family-owned quality store must leave the San Francisco scene, which it dominated for more than a century.*
>
> *We are solvent. No one can force us to go out of business. We are doing it voluntarily. There will be no bankruptcy or receivership. We shall honor all of our obligations, as we have in the past, and bow out in a dignified and honorable manner befitting our San Francisco tradition.*
>
> *Just like the motto on our crest, beneath the original City of Paris sailing ship—"Fluctuat nec Mergiture" (It may rock but never sinks)—City of Paris will not sink but will retire with grace, leaving in its wake 122 years of San Francisco tradition and memories.*
>
> *Thank you and Au Revoir.*[20]

THE TROOPS RALLY TO SAVE AN ICONIC BUILDING

The Verdier family might have said "Au revoir," but City of Paris and its beautiful building remained in the news for a decade. After the store closed in March 1972, Liberty House occupied the space until 1974, when its new store south of the City of Paris location was ready. Thus began an enormous planning fight, with historic preservationists on one side and the Texas firm of Neiman Marcus on the other.

Half of City of Paris's property in San Francisco was sold to Carter Hawley Hale Stores, which had acquired Neiman Marcus in 1969.

A flower vendor outside the City of Paris checks his blooms in the mid-1950s.
OpenSFHistory/wnp28.2358.jpg

Neiman Marcus claimed that when it bought the building, it had intended to keep the building intact, but then it was decided that it needed too many earthquake upgrades and the store required more selling space. Neiman Marcus then proposed tearing down the old store and replacing it with a $6 million structure designed by architect Philip Johnson (who replaced John Carl Warnecke).

Although the building was listed in the National Register of Historic Places and was a California State Landmark, the San Francisco Planning Commission denied landmark designation even though it was recommended by the Landmarks Commission. Over sixty thousand signatures were collected and passionate presentations made at the planning meetings.

But alas, the preservationists lost. On September 12, 1979, the San Francisco Board of Permit Appeals voted to allow the building to be torn down. Willie Brown, an attorney who went on to become mayor, represented Neiman Marcus. He said the historic building was an earthquake hazard and the Texas-based retailer should do what it wants with its property. The one concession Neiman Marcus made was to keep the rotunda and glass dome.

In the current Neiman Marcus store, architect Philip Johnson moved the rotunda and stained-glass skylight under a glass dome to the corner of the building that faces Union Square. *Peter Talke.*

Stanley Marcus, president of Neiman Marcus, also promised to continue the Christmas tree tradition.

As San Francisco's own Herb Caen put it during the last days of the store:

> *Feeling mellow, I walked over to the poor, doomed City of Paris, through the familiar doors, down the stairs to Normandie [sic] Lane, with its flavor of San Francisco French, books and magazines from Paris, good croissants, a decent pâté maison, and memories of debonair Paul Verdier, son of the founder, always twirling a glass of champagne between his fingers. Cultured, refined Monsieur Paul, as long-gone as the era that produced him and his kind and his kind of store.*[21]

Demolition began in 1980, and the new Neiman Marcus store with the rotunda and dome tucked inside opened in late 1982. The reception was lukewarm at best, illustrated by this article by Paul Goldberger, architecture critic at the *New York Times*:

> *Now that the building is done and the store is open, it is easy to see that the preservation-minded folk of this town knew wherefrom they spoke. For the Neiman Marcus building, even with the gracious rotunda preserved, is one of this city's most conspicuous architectural mistakes. It is an awkward intrusion into San Francisco, a building that struggles to reflect a certain spirit and ends up, instead, capturing that spirit under glass and nearly suffocating it.*
>
> *Neiman Marcus is a glittery, showy and altogether modern building; with its checkerboard facade and square windows punched out at asymmetrical points, it comes off as a disquieting mix of the sleek and the decorated.... The old seems trapped in the new, put on display in the front window as if it were a four-story-high jewel that Neiman Marcus had to sell, rather than a piece of architecture.*[22]

And so *La Ville de Paris*, the City of Paris ship, sailed away. Another icon of San Francisco history gone.

Chapter 2

THE WHITE HOUSE, 1854–1965

Raphael Weill, San Francisco's Merchant Prince

All the retail establishments had their stories. For the City of Paris, it was the Verdier family and the focus on all things French. For the White House, it was the story of Raphael Weill, its founder. Newspapers of the era are full of articles about Weill, a leading citizen and philanthropist who first arrived in San Francisco from France in 1854.

Born in Phalsbourg in the Lorraine region of northeastern France in 1837, Weill worked as an apprentice to a dry goods merchant in Metz before seeking his fortune in California. As the story goes, he sailed to the United States from Le Havre, France, in 1853, aboard the *Connecticut*, a packet boat bound for New York. In New York, he took off for Panama on the steamer *George Lowell*. Once in Panama, he boarded another boat headed to California, the *Golden Gate*, which was shipwrecked in San Diego.

Weill survived and made his way to San Francisco, arriving in January 1854. One newspaper, in the florid prose of the day, said he was "cast penniless on the beach in San Diego," but in an oral history,[23] Weill says he had friends and cousins in the city. He was related to the Lazards (Alexandre, Simon and Elie), three brothers from Alsace-Lorraine who had moved their dry goods establishment to San Francisco from New Orleans in 1851 and expanded into banking and foreign exchange as Lazard Frères & Co. Weill's brothers Sylvain, Jules, Henri and Alexander also resided in San Francisco, although it is unclear when they arrived.

In an interview,[24] Weill says that he went to the opera the night of his arrival in San Francisco—*Daughter of the Regiment* was playing at the Metropolitan Opera House.

The distinctive White House department store wrapped the corner of Grant Avenue and Sutter Street. *OpenSFHistory/wnp100.00008.jpg.*

Weill soon found employment with J.W. Davidson and Richard Lane of Davidson and Lane's at Sacramento and Kearny Streets. Davidson and Lane founded their small shop (reported to be twenty feet by forty feet) on June 19, 1854, which just happened to be the same week that the steamer *Brother Jonathan* arrived with 139 ladies on board, a welcome sight for the city that had many men seeking their fortunes but was sorely lacking female residents. The influx of women bode well for the new store.[25]

Once Weill joined the firm, a sign in the window announced, *Ici on parle Français.* At the time, San Francisco swarmed with Frenchmen, many of whom spoke very little English, so they were happy to find a store with a courteous, French-speaking staff member.

The fashionable street promenade…where one met friends and loitered through the shops, extended from Sutter Street along Montgomery to Clay, up Clay to Kearney [sic] Street and across the Plaza to Washington…. Along this route were the shops of Belloc Frères, the Ville de Paris, and at Sacramento and Kearney Streets, Davidson and Lane's, where Raphael Weill, a handsome black-eyed French boy whom everyone liked, was clerk.[26]

Weill rose rapidly. By 1858, he had replaced Lane, who left to seek his fortunes in the Fraser River gold fields. One newspaper article said that "by stretching his resources and drawing a little on credit, young Weill was able to finance the deal."[27] Yet another source[28] says that Weill's brother Alexander bought him a partnership. In any case, the name of the store became J.W. Davidson & Co., with "Co." being Weill, the junior partner.

A SAN FRANCISCO INSTITUTION

After its beginnings in the small store at Sacramento and Kearny Streets, the store relocated several times prior to the 1906 earthquake, each time to grander, more substantial space. In the mid-1860s, it moved to Montgomery and Post Streets, on the same block as the Lick House, a hotel built by James Lick in 1861 that was considered one of the finest hotels in the West. Its dining room could seat four hundred. By that time, Weill had established a buying agency in Paris, so the store was constantly supplied and San Francisco had some of the best-dressed women in the United States.

Soon, the firm decided to build a home of its own, a three-story brick structure at Kearny and Post Streets, which opened in 1870. Weill changed the name to the White House, after the store Maison Blanche in Paris. When the new store opened on December 7, 1870, it was considered top of the line. In 1885, J.W. Davidson retired and went home to England, and Weill became senior partner with his brother Henry and Eugene Gallois. In 1893, the firm was incorporated as Raphael Weill Inc., the entity that operated the store. Weill had come a long way from being shipwrecked, "penniless," on the San Diego shores.

Let's examine more closely Raphael Weill, the man, and the firm of Raphael Weill & Co., which operated the White House.

The White House opened in a new location in 1870 at the corner of Kearny and Post Streets, a fashionable shopping district. *California History Room, California State Library, Sacramento, California.*

The White House was known for its impeccable customer service. Here, salesmen in the glove and handkerchief department stand by to assist in 1899. *Raphael Weill papers and photographs, BANC MSS 2010/719, the Bancroft Library, University of California–Berkeley.*

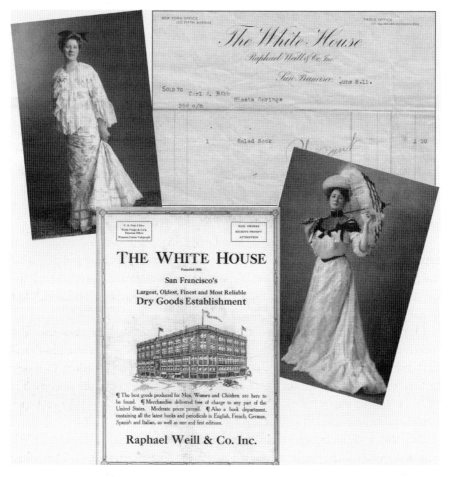

A fashionable lady (in a corset, of course) in the early 1900s wearing her lovely dresses from the White House. *Mark O'Neill, Kathleen Manning, author's collection.*

SAN FRANCISCO'S FIRST CITIZEN

Hail Raphael Weill, Son of France and America, Friend of Humanity, Upholder of Liberty and Right, Beloved Citizen of our City! San Francisco takes you into her heart in joy and thankfulness that you have returned sage and triumphant to her welcoming arms.

This effusive homage to Weill, an inscription on a gold plate presented to Weill upon his return in 1919 after three years in France doing relief work, is only one of many tributes Weill received over the years. Articles regularly appeared in the local papers with titles such as "France Honors Raphael Weill: Well-Known Merchant Is Made Chevalier of Legion of Honor," "Weill Celebrates His 75th Birthday: White House Employes [*sic*] Present Silver Book and Stand to Proprietor," "Raphael Weill Resident Here 59 Years Friday," "Raphael Weill 80 Years Old: Congratulations Are Cabled, Veteran Merchant Prince Gives $10,000 to San Francisco Charities on His Birthday," "Spontaneous Ovations Greeted Raphael Weill, Veteran Merchant and Philanthropist, on His Return," "Weill Celebrates 66th Anniversary of Landing in U.S.: Formal Opening of New Tea Room with Reception to Employes [*sic*] Commemorates Event" and "Raphael Weill Honored on His 83rd Birthday."

Weill was a great believer in the power of the media, which probably had something to do with the publication of these stories. "Tell the public, show the public, don't keep it as secret,"[29] he constantly drummed into the ears of his associates. "The public—all the public read newspapers," he said. "Let us use them."

One of the often-repeated stories about Weill is that he was the first merchant to request a full-page ad in a newspaper, which was considered outlandish at the time, and he was turned down by the publisher. Not one to take defeat lightly, he just kept asking until the paper finally accepted it in 1874, publishing what was supposedly the first full-page ad printed in an American newspaper.

But the headlines above are about more than public relations. Weill was a popular figure, one of San Francisco's leading citizens. Outgoing and personable, he not only gave money and time to various causes, but he was also beloved by his employees. Weill maintained a large staff and selected his employees carefully. He regarded speed and courtesy as the foundation of good salesmanship, believing that customers kept waiting would become cross and less likely to spend. As Gertrude Atherton recounted in *My San Francisco*:

> *He was a rather short stout man with a beaming intelligent face. One rarely entered the White House without meeting him, for he knew all his customers personally and liked to chat with them. I cannot remember how many times he informed me that he had known five generations of my family, but he* [then] *liked to divert the conversation to France, to which he was still devoted with his heart if not with his honest and enterprising head.*[30]

During World War I, when many of his employees were drafted, Weill put half their salaries into an account for a year while they were serving. According to a 1920 article written the day after his death,[31] the White House was considered one of the most desirable places to work in the city. He referred to his employees as "co-workers" rather than "employees." "I attribute my business success almost entirely to my confidence in my employees. I never call them employees, however. I prefer to think of them as co-workers, for without their aid and co-operation my business would be impossible."[32]

The night Weill returned from France in 1919, eight hundred employees met him at the Ferry Building with a banner saying his co-workers welcomed him home. To travel to a public reception honoring him at city hall, Weill was escorted from the St. Francis Hotel by hundreds of mounted and marching policemen and firemen. "Traffic was stopped and the Municipal Band played when he took his place in a gaily decorated auto, bearing French and American flags and completely covered with red carnations and greenery."[33]

Raphael Weill, founder of the White House, arrived in San Francisco in 1854 and went on to become a leading merchandiser and citizen. *California History Room, California State Library, Sacramento, California.*

The White House was very generous to its "co-worker" employees and was known for its gentility and square dealings, which employees appreciated, understandably. In an era when labor policies were not as well defined as they are now, the White House instituted its own generous benefits: all employees got all holidays off, vacation with pay, paid sick leave and a commission on their sales in addition to a salary. The employees entered and exited the front door of the store, same as the customers. The store was the first to close at the civilized hour of 6:00 p.m. "'Cherish me. Take good care of me, and I'll take good care of you. I'm your job,'" was the closing line in an editorial in an employee newsletter.

Another example of Weill's generosity is an often-cited story about something he did after the 1906 earthquake, when he quietly ordered a shipment of five thousand dresses and undergarments—sixteen thousand items total—to be brought around the Horn and distributed to female refugees who were displaced because of the fire. A table was set up near the store's temporary quarters. In his office, he kept a silver loving cup that had been presented to him by the recipients of the clothing, along with a book containing 250 names of the grateful recipients.

Despite his popularity, Weill shunned running for public office, as he was not interested in being a politician. His only foray into that kind of public service was when he ran as a candidate for the school board because it had such a corrupt reputation and he wanted to do something about it. He served two terms.[34]

Even though Weill was such a popular public figure, it's difficult to find much about his personal life. Described as the perfect Frenchman, a "boulevardier, club man, arts patron and connoisseur, gourmet chef and perennially eligible bachelor"[35] man about town, he loved to cook for his friends.

An active member of the Bohemian Club, the exclusive San Francisco men's club founded in 1872, he lodged for many years at the club's headquarters and was known for cooking up gourmet Sunday breakfasts for twenty-five or thirty friends. Heaven forbid if one should arrive late, as the "breakfast" (which could last for three hours) started at 12:00 p.m. sharp. A banquet in his honor in 1907 at the club listed "Alligator Pear Salad à la Raphael Weill" on the menu and "Chicken Raphael Weill," which was chicken with heavy cream, egg yolks and a dash of sherry wine, another of his popular concoctions.

In his oral history,[36] when asked direct questions about his family and religion, Weill was not as gregarious and forthcoming as he usually was portrayed in newspaper articles. His answer to the question, "Who was your father?" was "My father, but you are not going to put him in; what has he to do with this?" And regarding his mother, he said, "No, no, I do not care to give that….We came here as adventurers and without a family. We were the Argonauts."

And despite being part of the Jewish community in San Francisco (in the late nineteenth century, between 5 and 10 percent of San Francisco's Jewish population had its roots in Alsace or Lorraine),[37] he was not forthcoming at all when asked about his parents' religion: "No, no. You cannot get anything out of me about my parents. I do not see that it matters whether they were Jews, or Mohammedans or Christians….I decline to answer that on the same ground as the other. That is private."

Until 1914, Weill's life was his store and his Bohemian Club friends. (Asked in the oral history interview if he had a partner, he answered, "No sir, never. I am unmarried, and, worse than that, I am a bachelor, a confirmed bachelor.") He also kept his French connections, visiting France every year (he is buried in France).

However, a small newspaper article appeared in 1914: "Weill Quits S.F. Club as Nephew Is Barred as Member."[38] Anti-Semitism was on the rise, and although Weill was a founding member of the Bohemian Club, which had admitted numerous Jewish pioneers and their sons, by the pre–World War I era, attitudes were changing. When Michel Weill, Raphael's nephew (he had six) and heir, was rejected, Weill angrily resigned. No more mentions appeared in newspapers of gala dinners he hosted at the club. In later years, he had an apartment at the St. Francis Hotel on Union Square.

1906 FIRE DESTROYS DOWNTOWN

The 1906 earthquake and fire destroyed downtown San Francisco, and the White House building was ruined, along with many of the records and ledgers (except those that the faithful White House delivery wagon was able to save). With Weill's usual resilience, he opened a temporary store at the northwest corner of Van Ness Avenue and Pine Street by late July. All employees who had been employed in April prior to the earthquake and fire were employed and at their stations in the temporary store. Meanwhile, Weill and his partners set about building an even grander new store.

As San Francisco and its citizens struggled in the months after the fire, they truly appreciated having stores stocked with goods to replenish their homes and lift their spirits. Julia Altrocchi describes the scene at Christmas the year of the earthquake: "Of all the holiday seasons that San Francisco had ever enjoyed, that of December, 1906, and January, 1907, now seemed the very gayest. Shreve's and The White House were swarming with customers."[39]

By 1909, the new store at Sutter and Grant was ready to open. Designed by noted architect Albert Pissis, who also designed the Hibernia Bank Building, Flood Building and the Emporium, it was a massive, four-story structure with a steel frame and a white (of course) exterior of terra cotta, with cast-iron elements and wood windows. The huge structure, decorated with French and American flags for its opening, occupied over half the

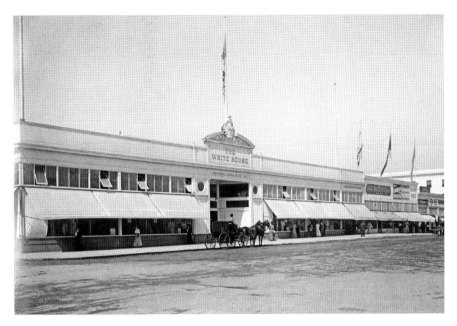

By late July after the April earthquake, Weill had opened a temporary store at the northwest corner of Van Ness Avenue and Pine Street. *California History Room, California State Library, Sacramento, California.*

length of the block on two frontages. On its grand opening day, March 13, 1909, automobiles lined up for blocks to drop people off as thousands came to see the elegant new store. "White House Charms Throngs and Marks City's Recovery"[40] shouted a *San Francisco Call* headline on March 14, 1909.

> *To the city of San Francisco the inauguration at the White House last night had all the significance that a presidential inauguration has to the nation. It was the inauguration of the newer, greater, grander San Francisco. It marked the return downtown of the great bulk of the stores that had been swept away in the big fire. They have been coming back in greater or less degree for months.... The new White House is far bigger and finer in every way than it was before the fire. One million dollars is invested in the building and hundreds of thousands more in a stock of goods that for rarity and artistic standards is unexcelled in the fashion marts of America.*[41]

WHY WAS THE STORE SPECIAL?

From its early days, the White House was known for smart merchandising and graciousness. Raphael Weill set the tone for courtesy and customer service. Ladies in carriages could sit at the curb, and clerks would bring goods out for their inspection. Agents in New York and Paris made sure the store was stocked with the latest styles of woolen fabrics, silks, linens, mourning goods, laces, hosiery, fancy goods and haberdashery. In the days before ready-to-wear clothing became available, an 1872 article noted that on the store's third floor, over 100 people were employed to produce "every mentionable and unmentionable article of ladies' attire in the latest and most improved fashion and should the case be urgent, with immediate rapidity."[42] By the 1880s, a co-worker known affectionately as "Mademoiselle Max" was in charge of 150 seamstresses in the dressmaking department. "Ladies who have lived in San Francisco and are now residing in New York still send to the White House for their dresses."[43]

And just in case you wanted that extra special something, located in the upper corner of the store there was a dark room, lit by gas in the daytime, so female customers could see how the colors of the silks and satins they were considering would look under the gaslight. After trying on your dress, you could retire to the tearoom, the Salon de Thé, on the fourth floor, with its smoky-mirrored walls, lush green plants and flowers and French cuisine.

Lolita "Lolly" Erlanger, who worked at the store as a teenager in 1942–43 through a program with her high school, was fascinated by the White House's glove department. "When you wanted to buy gloves, you placed your elbow on a little pad and then the saleswoman would work the leather glove over your hands." (An early store ad touted the glove department: "Great Glove counter, the Sole Agency of the Celebrated Preville Kid Glove.") Lolly worked on the main floor, in the fragrance department selling cologne, soap and perfume, while "floorwalkers"—men in business suits with white boutonnieres—would make their rounds just to make sure everything was running smoothly.

A fleet of distinctive White House delivery trucks (white, of course) traveled throughout the city for many years delivering goods (some 28,346,600 packages over the years, according to a company brochure) to customers. During World War II, the trucks were outfitted to be ambulances, if necessary. In 1946, the store let UPS take over, citing more efficient service for customers and less traffic congestion in the city. All White House drivers were guaranteed a job at the same salary.

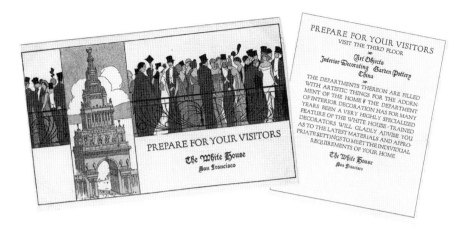

Millions of visitors flocked to San Francisco in 1915 for the Panama-Pacific International Exposition. The White House offered its decorating services for those customers expecting guests. *C035228. The Society of California Pioneers.*

In 1947, "Babette," a fashion columnist in the *San Francisco Examiner*, announced breathlessly that the White House Teen Shop was opening and that "teen-agers are about to have a shop that is really and truly their very own." The teens helped plan it, "and what's more, they're going to help RUN the shop. Teenagers will be on the 'advisory council.'…They will act as sales people…model in fashion shows…serve as hostesses."[44]

What a clever marketing strategy—280 teens answered a four-page questionnaire and got to vote on what they wanted in the store, from decorations to fashion shows. They responded with their favorite magazines, actresses, singers, music, color, nail polish shade and lipstick color. You can image the excitement when the Teen Shop opened. In 1964, an article[45] appeared saying it was tryout time for the Teen Board, which required good grooming and neat appearance, a well-proportioned figure, leadership qualities, an active school record and fashion interest. Those chosen would get to model in fashion shows and participate in beauty clinics and fashion seminars. This was a savvy way to get the target market involved.

Always on the lookout for ways to draw customers to the store, the White House—one of thirty-four participating organizations—became a farmers' market during a ten-day Harvest Festival in the fall of 1963 and 1964. Thirty of the store's windows featured California's agricultural products, and members of the 4-H Clubs and Future Farmers of America assisted more than thirty farmers in staffing thirty-four produce booths and stalls on the sidewalks.

Left: A street photographer snapped this photo of Vera Coates walking in front of the White House in the 1930s. *Tricia Mack.*

Below: A happy little girl shows off her White House "auto" in the 1930s. *Francesca Pera.*

Howard Greer dramatizes navy wool with white embroidery. Ours exclusively in San Francisco.

THE WHITE HOUSE
RAPHAEL WEILL & COMPANY
SAN FRANCISCO

Top: Order your new embroidered navy wool dress, and one of the White House delivery trucks would bring it to your door. *Author's collection.*

Bottom: Long ago, in the days before plastic shopping bags, customers brought their goods home in a distinctive White House box. *Ron Ross.*

The White House's selling space was spread out over four buildings; this is a view of the store at Post Street and Grant Avenue in the late '50s. *OpenSFHistory/wnp28.2437.jpg.*

Arthur Corbin, who was one of the 4-H kids who worked the festival, said that the 4-H members traveled by bus from the Central Valley, and when they arrived, they were given a pair of Levi's jeans and a plaid shirt. From almonds to zucchini, the booths highlighted the many fruits and vegetables grown in California.

In 1961, Lucinda Larsen, the "Wizard of Ooze" and grandmother of fifteen, demonstrated her frosting techniques at the Housewares Fair at the White House. "Her deft hand—'it's all in the wrist action'—turn out a fairyland fantasy in frosting, a three-foot high wedding cake or a simple 'Happy Birthday' scroll with equal ease."[46]

SO WHAT HAPPENED?

By the mid-twentieth century, the store had lost its cachet. Without Weill's driving personality, the store seemed to lose its distinctiveness. His nephew Michel Weill was president until 1960 but retired without a firm succession plan. A group of investors, California Century Stores, put together by investment banking firm William Blair & Co., bought 90 percent of the stock in Raphael Weill & Co. in 1958. The new owners hired new executives, and the following two years were very profitable, but after that, the store's fortunes declined rapidly.

The decision to open a branch store in the Kaiser Center in Oakland in mid-1960 turned out poorly; the branch never recouped its $2 million start-up cost, and the big loss and working capital inadequacies affected the San Francisco store's efforts to spruce up and restore its slipping prestige image. The store didn't keep up with its competitors that were branching out to the suburbs; the White House lost its customers to those stores.

The huge store, composed of four buildings with four landlords and leases, faced big problems in downtown San Francisco because of its inefficient and inconvenient merchandising layout, according to a *Women's Wear Daily* article: "Different floor levels, poor communications, difficult traffic patterns—both between floors and on individual floors, low ratio of usable selling space and low efficiency of the selling space, much of which was in corners, which again hampered traffic flow."[47]

By January 1965, after 111 years, it was over. Imagine this scene on January 26, the beginning of an eleven-day, 25 percent off sale to raise cash. Cash only, all sales final, no alterations. It was bedlam. Lines went out the door, and special officers had to turn people away because of fire department regulations. Sixteen Pinkerton guards were in the store, and special cashier booths were set up on all five floors for the endless stream of shoppers who waited as long as forty-five minutes to make their purchases. "It's like watching a grand old lady die," a woman in a mink coat said, "and nobody remembering how lovely she was once."[48]

When it was all over, gross proceeds from the sale totaled $2 million. But it wasn't enough. Bankruptcy debts totaled $8,565,642 and assets were $8,442,347. San Francisco mayor John Shelley held a meeting the day after the sale to try to come up with a plan to save the store. If the store closed, San Francisco would lose a major downtown presence, and 850 employees, many who had worked there for over twenty years and some for over forty, would lose their jobs. The White House filed for bankruptcy three days after the cash sale ended. To help save the store, financier Louis Lurie offered $6 million in February to keep the store open and allow the store to buy the four properties on which it was located. His plan was to then buy back the properties for $7 million, giving the White House $1 million in profit. Unfortunately, the store needed close to $10 million to keep from sinking.

In a Sunday paper soon after closing, an ad stated, "The White House is closed. Thank you for your patronage and your loyalty over the years." And in smaller type: "For the payment of bills, please use the Post Street entrance."

It was a long road down from the store's heyday. Fifty-nine years earlier, founder Raphael Weill said, "Men come and go. The personnel of the store changes with time, but the White House will go on, I believe, indefinitely."[49] But alas, that was not to be. However, the loyal employees still stayed in touch as best they could. In 1984, almost twenty years after the store closed, there were three hundred former employees who occasionally got together to reminisce about those good old days.

Chapter 3

GUMP'S, 1861–2018

"Good Taste Costs No More"

During most of the past century, when a young woman in San Francisco got engaged, it was just assumed that she would register for her wedding gifts at Gump's, known by its marketing tag line, "Good Taste Costs No More." Although other stores carried china and silver, Gump's was known as *the* place to find everything to set an elegant table. On the second floor of its flagship store at 250 Post Street, very knowledgeable salespeople would lead the newly engaged woman through the myriad china offerings, from Lenox and Wedgwood to Hutschenreuther, Herend, Ceralene and Haviland. A full room was dedicated to Baccarat crystal. The silver room (103 designs) featured antique silver but also contemporary designs.

Of all the stores featured in this book, Gump's held on the longest, closing in late 2018. That year, the sad "going out of business" signs were in every window of the 135 Post Street location, where it had moved in 1995. Walking through the store in its last days, perusing the piles of Christmas ornaments, Mikasa place settings and racks of discounted clothes, I was struck by how the store was just a shadow of its former glory. Three generations of Gumps— Solomon and Gustave, Abraham Livingston "A.L." and Richard—steered the store from its early beginnings in 1861 selling gilded frames, mirrors and art to the newly rich of the gold rush to its mid-century glory featuring Asian and other choice, carefully curated items from around the world. The family sold the store in 1969, Richard Gump retired in 1974 and various other owners tried to make a go of it, maintaining its robust catalogue business, but once again, the changing retail landscape and shopping habits (registering on Etsy for wedding gifts?) were too much to overcome.

A PIONEER ART DEALER

Solomon Gump did not arrive along with all the gold seekers; he arrived in California in 1863. He had been in the United States since 1850, arriving as a seventeen-year-old in New York with his brother Gustave from Heidelberg, Germany, where their father was a cultured linen merchant. Solomon worked as a ship chandler, a retail dealer who specializes in supplies or equipment for ships, in Apalachicola, Florida, and then joined the Confederate army for a few months. He soon made the move to California, arriving by Pacific Mail steamer in the spring of 1863 to meet up with his sister Gertrude and her husband, David Haussmann. Haussmann had started a business, David Haussmann & Co., a few years prior, selling mirrors for the many saloons in town and gilded cornices for the newly minted millionaires' mansions. Business was good, and

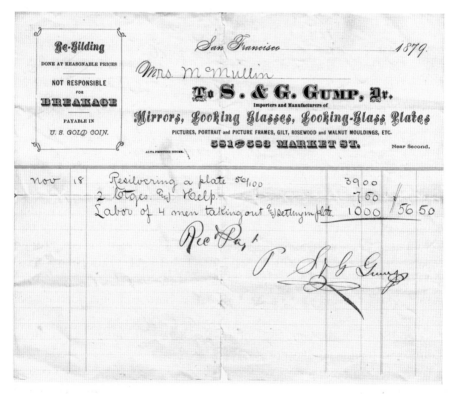

In 1879, a Mrs. McMullin paid a grand total of $56.50 to have a plate re-silvered by S. & G. Gump, who specialized in gilt, mirrors and looking-glass plates. *Ron Ross.*

Solomon, anxious to make his fortune, saw possibilities. He purchased an interest in Haussmann's shop, located at 535–37 Clay Street, wanting to get established quickly so his wife, Louisa, and young children could join him. Louisa was reluctant to come west to the raucous, fast-growing city, with its lack of refined social life compared to the more rarified atmosphere of the East.

By 1864, Solomon had bought Haussmann out and went into business with his brother Gustave, who had made his way west along with Louisa and family. S. & G. Gump was born.

In those Barbary Coast days, San Franciscans gathered with their cohorts in saloons lavishly decorated with large gilt-framed mirrors and huge paintings, often of nudes. Barroom brawls and flying bullets meant that mirrors needed to be replaced frequently. S. & G. Gump found its first profitable niche.

Soon they were selling more than mirrors and frames; they were becoming art dealers as well. As A.L. Gump, Solomon's son, recounted in a *Saturday Evening Post* article:

> *San Francisco was an art dealer's idea of heaven on earth in the late bonanza days. The town was exhilarated with easily made wealth. Nob Hill was crowded with the mansions of newborn millionaires. Those who had just acquired wealth were trying to keep up with the Stanfords, the Huntingtons, the Crockers, the Fairs, the Floods, the Mackays. The race to acquire art and culture was on. Those were great days!*[50]

Solomon traveled to Europe to search out works of art for their new venture, the first art gallery in California. He had an eye for what his clientele wanted, from romantic landscapes to voluptuous nudes. Richard Gump, Solomon's grandson, said that it wasn't that Solomon had such great taste in art; the nudes were actually of Solomon's lady friend, a European actress. Wife Louisa refused to have the paintings in the house. He also brought Louisa gifts from Europe: "As a result of his European philanderings Sol surfeited Mrs. Gump with presents. Rumor has it that one day she'd had enough. She sent the chotchkas off to the store with orders to sell them. Gump's was in the gift business."[51]

As business grew, the store moved to various locations in the last decades of the nineteenth century. From its original location on Clay Street, it moved to 117–19 Sansome Street (with a factory on Market Street), then to Market Street in 1876 and then to 113–15 Geary Boulevard, near Union Square,

An early ad for S. & G. Gump: "Manufacturers and importers of mirrors, window cornices, pictures and frames, mouldings, looking-glass plates, Etc., Etc." *California History Room, California State Library, Sacramento, California.*

in 1892. After the Gilded Age of the 1870s and 1880s, San Francisco and the rest of the United States suffered during the economic turmoil of the 1893 depression, when railroads, banks and mercantile houses went under. Nevada silver mines shut down and unemployed miners streamed into the city. Gump's survived by auctioning off artworks and finding investors to help with its debts.

A.L., MASTER MERCHANT

Of Solomon and Louisa's eight children (Henrietta, Isabella, Lafayette, Alfred S., Sigmund, Abraham Livingston "A.L.," Goldina and William Edgar), only A.L., born in 1869, showed serious interest in the store. As a young boy, he often went with his father to wealthy customers' homes and learned the intricacies of the business and art appreciation. These skills were to prove especially useful as he began to lose his eyesight to glaucoma at eleven years old. He finally left school at thirteen and went to work in his father's store. A.L. and two of his brothers, Alfred and William, took over the store from Solomon and Gustave in the early 1900s. Solomon's health was failing, and it was time for him to step aside (he died in 1908). A.L., despite his limited eyesight, propelled the store into a new era, when the store and the name "Gump's" became internationally renowned for its jade and Asian art collections.

On that fateful day in 1906, as the city burned after the earthquake, the store on Geary was ruined. All the art burned except for a few bronzes, which looters took. A.L. cabled his brother Alfred, who was on a buying trip in Europe, telling him to cancel orders and come home. Most of Alfred's purchases had been shipped already, however, which was fortunate as it soon became clear there was going to be high demand.

A.L. was determined to rebuild. The store's insurance was mostly with German firms, which refused to pay at first because they said it was the earthquake and not the fire that caused the damage, which wasn't true. (It took some San Francisco merchants of German descent to travel to Germany to convince the insurance companies to pay up.) Legend has it that A.L. turned to Dodie Valencia, a wealthy art collector and a woman of questionable reputation known as the "Toast of the Coast," who offered A.L. $17,000 for a painting from his private collection, and that got the enterprise going again.

Like other department stores displaced by the fire, Gump's set up temporary headquarters near Van Ness Avenue, at 1645 California Street between Van Ness and Polk Street, until it could move back to Union Square. By 1909, the store had returned to Union Square by leasing, and eventually buying, a building designed by well-known architect Clinton Day at 250 Post Street, where the store was to remain until it relocated in 1995. Business was good, according to A.L.:

> *If ever there was a paradox, it was San Francisco rising from the ruins. No sooner had the burned-out citizens of the town collected their insurance than they began to look for ways to spend their money. Gaiety and optimism abounded. Wages were high and everybody had more business than he could possibly handle. The town was rolling in ready cash....For every millionaire bonanza king who had been a prospective patron of the arts before the catastrophe, there were now twenty contractors or merchants or draymen whose wives were seeking the finest things they could buy.*[52]

After the earthquake, as the store started acquiring new stock, A.L. pushed for featuring goods from the Far East. His brothers wanted to restrict

Japanese artist Chiura Obata's striking ceiling mural adorned the Lotus Room, one of the "Oriental" rooms A.L. Gump created in anticipation of visitors to the Pan-Pacific International Exposition. *Author's collection.*

their merchandise to objects of proven worth, the works of art that had appealed to San Francisco's "new money" for years. A.L. was influenced by his wife, Mabel, a successful actress who was interested in the teachings of Professor Ernest Fenollosa, an American art historian who lectured about the significance of Asian arts. A.L. saw Gump's future profits coming from across the Pacific, despite the public's widely held "anti-Oriental" prejudice. (The Chinese Exclusion Act prohibiting immigration of Chinese laborers was passed in 1882 and extended with the Geary Act in 1902.) He wanted to team up with Ed Newell, a buyer with experience in the field. A.L. finally convinced his brothers that one-third of the temporary store would become an "Oriental Room," while two-thirds of the store could be devoted to European imports. Newell and A.L. displayed their first few pieces on an altar Newell had salvaged from a burned-out Buddhist temple. Millionaire George Crocker was one of the first customers, and word spread quickly. As Richard Gump said in his book, *Jade: Stone of Heaven*:

> *The Oriental department of Gump's was an immediate success—demand for fine porcelains, paintings, kimonos, embroidered brocades, lacquer and teakwood often exceeded the supply, though soldiers and marines returning from China after the Boxer Rebellion provided an unexpected source of Asian art.*[53]

Newell began making regular buying trips to Asia and soon had extensive contacts who taught him how to recognize the lesser-quality goods made for export. Newell sought out rare, genuine pieces, and his search often took him to remote villages. Newell and A.L. realized that some items such as Imperial Chinese rugs were beyond the reach of some Gump's customers, so why not make their own reproductions? Soon Gump's had a rug-making studio; designers sent watercolor designs to China, and artisans there got to work. San Francisco homes featured Japanese and Chinese prints on the walls instead of the gold-framed mirrors and marble statues of the late 1800s, as well as Japanese screens designed to complement a room's color palette and custom teakwood furniture. Hostesses draped a Chinese mandarin coat or a Japanese priest robe on pianos.

Jade was the next treasure to capture Newell's attention. He had seen some of it in San Francisco's Chinatown shops, but those goods were targeted at local Chinese customers. He believed there wasn't much interest among his California customers for the jade and jade carvings that Chinese artisans had produced for centuries. But the beauty of the carvings and their

A Buddha at Gump's serenely sits among fine old carved jades, statues, rare porcelains, bowls, rugs and paintings in this image from the late 1930s. *Devin Frick.*

color intrigued him. A.L Gump had an affectionate term for a weakness for jade: "jade madness." In the clutches of that state of mind, Newell brought some Ch'ien Lung (circa 1711–99) vases back to the store. Jade madness was contagious, and soon Newell was back in China seeking the finest jades for the growing demand in San Francisco.

A.L. had an extraordinary tactile sensitivity, perhaps developed because of his limited sight. He became a leading authority on jade, carrying with him a small piece of high-quality jade so he could compare it to other jades. He made his first trip to China with Newell in 1917 and learned the ins and outs of the buying process in Asia (don't wear your best clothes; bid low and argue; and disguise your enthusiasm when offered something extraordinary).

Gump's became known for its fine jade, and Newell's purchases became the inspiration for establishing the Jade Room on Post Street. The Jade Room joined other rooms that displayed all of the Gump's treasures to maximum advantage. Needing more space and in anticipation of the upcoming Panama-Pacific International Exposition (PPIE) in 1915, they expanded into an annex to the Post Street building where, in addition to the Jade Room, they could feature their treasures in other rooms devoted to lacquer, porcelain, bronze and kimonos.

COMING TO THE FAIR

In 1915, San Francisco was ready to prove to the world that the city had more than recovered from the earthquake and fire of 1906. The PPIE, a world's fair to celebrate the completion of an engineering marvel, the Panama Canal, opened in late February. It was a greater success than expected, with over eighteen million visitors over nine months. Many included a visit to Gump's, where A.L. made sure there were fresh flowers every day (including the red carnation boutonniere he always wore) and the visitors, who often were unfamiliar with Asian art, received first-class treatment from knowledgeable employees. Emily Post (the future etiquette expert), who had driven to San Francisco from the East Coast to attend the fair, wrote of her visit (at the insistence of a friend) to Gump's:

> *Feeling very much bored at being kept away from the Exposition, I entered a store reminiscent of a dozen in New York, walked down an aisle lined on either side with commonplace chinaware. My first sensation of boredom was changing to irritability. Then we entered an elevator and in the next instant I took back everything I had been thinking. It was as though we had been transported, not only across the Pacific, but across centuries of time. Through the apartments of an ancient Chinese palace, we walked into a Japanese temple, and again into a room in a modern Japanese house. You do not need more than a first glance to appreciate why they lead visitors to a shop with the unpromising name of Gump….In this museum-shop each room has been assembled as a setting for the things that are shown in it. Old Chinese porcelains, blue and white, sang de boeuf, white, apple-green, cucumber-green and peacock-blue, are shown in a room of the Ming Period in ebony and gold lacquer. The windows of all the rooms, whether in the walls or ceiling, are of translucent porcelain in the Chinese, or paper in the Japanese, which produces an indescribable illusion of having left the streets of San Francisco thousands of miles, instead of merely a few feet, behind you.*[54]

An eighteenth-century Buddha greets visitors at the entrance to the Far Eastern wing of the store. *Author's collection.*

A.L. was not only a shrewd judge of jade by touch, but he was also adept at showing important visitors around the store and commenting on each object without giving away his visual limitation. The guest book listed names such as actress Sarah Bernhardt (who bought a tiny iron snake that she said she would use when she played Cleopatra), Lily Langtry and Franklin Roosevelt (ship models and a dinner jacket) and Eleanor Roosevelt (jade after-dinner cups and saucers as a wedding gift for the Duchess of Kent). Once A.L.'s attentiveness backfired, however, when an actress sauntered out of the store assuming a necklace was a gift from A.L., as Carol Wilson describes in her *Gump's Treasure Trade*:

> [A.L.] *had a phrase that usually proved irresistible. "Now I really want you to have this," he would say as he discoursed on the appropriateness of a jade ring to a charming woman, a rare porcelain to a connoisseur or an antique desk to a tycoon. But experience taught him to follow through adroitly with more sales talk after one visiting actress, a really good customer, took him literally when he asked her to pose before the mirror wearing a beautiful jade necklace—"so perfect for you," he said, "I had you in mind when I first laid eyes on it. I really want you to have it."*

"Thank you kindly, Mr. Gump," she replied, with the gracious air of one accustomed to expensive gifts from admirers. "It will always be a reminder of our friendship." And she walked out of the store resplendent with her costly token.[55]

In the aftermath of World War I, the store continued to prosper. Prior to the war, 1915, the year of the PPIE, had been one of the best. Postwar, 1928 was a stellar year. By the late '20s, A.L. and his brother Alfred had parted ways (A.L. bought Alfred out). And although another brother, William "Willie," was still involved, A.L. was in charge, ruling the store like a beneficent despot, turning his charm on and off as needed.

ALOHA, WAIKIKI

Soon the lure of the Hawaiian Islands beckoned when a Hawaii resident, interior designer and landscaper Alice Spalding Bowen, came up with the idea of opening a Gump's store in the islands. In 1923, during a trip to San Francisco, she dropped by A.L.'s office to propose it to him. A.L. and his elder son, Robert, began considering opening a Gump's outpost in Honolulu.

Waikiki was a vacation paradise, with hula dancers, bronzed beach boys and very limited commercial development. A lot close to the elegant Royal Hawaiian hotel became available, and by February 1929, Gump's had opened at the corner of Kalakaua Avenue and Lewers Street. Architect Hart Wood created a structure that combined Chinese style with Hawaiian flavor. (The building was added to the National Register of Historic Places in 1973.) The store attracted affluent tourists and residents with its white stucco exterior walls, imperial blue tiled roof, jade-colored carpets and courtyards with pools, pomegranate bushes, statues of cranes and Chinese, Japanese and native plants.

When visitors walked into the Jade Room on the second floor, the first thing they would see would be a huge ancient lock from the Imperial Palace in Peking. Throughout the store there were the treasures Gump's was known for: museum-quality Asian art objects, old porcelains, jades, ancient bronzes, burial pottery, vases and primitive items. Gump's pioneered using local crafts created just for the store, such as glassware etched with Hawaiian flowers and koa bowls. The store was a big hit, and A.L. loved his Pacific outpost.

Gump's Hawaiian outpost at the corner of Kalakaua Avenue and Lewers Street. Architect Hart Wood's structure combined Chinese style with Hawaiian flavor. *Hawaii State Archives.*

Locals and tourists alike flocked to the Waikiki Gump's, which featured courtyards with pools, statues of cranes and Chinese, Japanese and native plants. *Hawaii State Archives.*

Little did A.L. suspect what was to come later that year. Even though the Hawaiian store had had a strong start, the stock market crash meant that visitors no longer had the discretionary income to flock to the golden sands of Waikiki, and the big spenders on the mainland also cut back.

A.L. was determined to stick with it for the long term. He had been through other crashes and knew that someday there would be a recovery. For the present, he needed to concentrate on selling what he could to high-end clients who could still afford it and collecting unpaid debts as much as he could. The store survived.

AN EYE FOR DESIGN

During World War II, the store turned to Mexico, Africa, the South Seas and other countries for goods, as its usual sources overseas were in areas affected by the conflict and not friendly to U.S. merchants. A.L.'s son Richard, who became vice president and general manager in 1944, worked to adapt local crafts to appeal to a more modern sensibility. Richard became more and more involved with the store, although as a child, he had not shown much promise or interest. His father said he was too artistic and impractical to be a businessman. Richard proved his father wrong, however, and had his own distinct approach to merchandising, which he was able to put into practice after A.L.'s death in 1947. Richard became president in 1947, and his older brother Robert, who was more shy, introspective and less of a salesman than Richard and A.L., resigned in 1948.

But before Richard could put his own stamp on Gump's, he had to deal with the reality of settling A.L.'s estate and crushing inheritance taxes and legal issues. Everything that A.L. owned personally that hadn't been included in his will went on the auction block to raise cash. And Richard made the very difficult decision in 1951 to close the Hawaii outpost. They needed the cash, not only to settle A.L.'s estate but also to help develop the mother ship in San Francisco so it could grow to accommodate the Bay Area's postwar burgeoning population. A smaller shop in Carmel, California (where the Gump family had a home), also closed. In making these difficult decisions, Richard Gump showed that he had the business acumen needed to move the store forward.

How to describe Richard Benjamin Gump? He was a witty and handsome artist, musician, serious composer, writer, designer, bon vivant, merchant and

Richard Gump—composer, artist, writer and lecturer—led the store for over twenty years. His "Good Taste Costs No More" slogan became the defining theme for the store. *San Francisco History Center, San Francisco Public Library.*

lecturer. And let's not forget conductor of the Guckenheimer Sour Kraut Band, whose members ("Ludwig Schmitz," "Johann Sebastian Schmidtz, III," "Otto Schmits" and other "Schm…" variations) wore ill-fitting military uniforms that looked like they were from the Franco-Prussian War. Richard liked to have a silly outlet because he found the art world he encountered at his day job at Gump's could be very stuffy.

The band played at charity fundraisers and festivals, and despite their off-key "music," TV hosts such as Arthur Godfrey, Ernie Ford and Arlene Francis featured them on their shows. Their music, played on a tuba, flugelhorn, trombone, clarinet and cornet—out of tune and a little out of tempo—was limited to sharp flats and flat sharps. Luckily, three albums—*Music for Non-Thinkers, Sour Kraut in Hi-Fi* and *Ommpah-pah in Hi-Fi*—preserved their old-fashioned German beer-drinking music for posterity.

When Richard was young, he wanted to be a big-league baseball player. A childhood accident and a long recuperation dashed that dream but gave him time to sketch and explore other avenues. Educated at the California College of Arts and Crafts and Stanford University, Richard tried different career paths in Hollywood for nearly a decade: draftsman, actor's agent, set designer and composer. Yet he eventually made his way back to the family business, and he was the one who managed to widen the store's appeal with his "Good Taste Costs No More" strategy.

APPEALING TO A WIDER AUDIENCE

In A.L.'s day, there were the very wealthy, the very poor and only a small middle ground. After World War II, that curve changed, and a bigger middle class emerged while the very wealthy and very poor populations decreased. Richard wanted to play down the store's snob appeal and attract that middle group, but not at the expense of good design. At Gump's, under Richard's watchful eye, whether an item was $5 or $10,000, it would be in good taste.

Richard laid out his goals for employees in a 1944 memo: good taste, originality whenever possible and knowledge of merchandise. As he recalled in his oral history:

> I inherited this high-speed horse.…I didn't want to just keep him in the barn, I wanted to let him run. So if I had certain ideas about how to make this horse win, I didn't want to be stopped. Fortunately I was head of the place and I could really let the horse go. I chose to be as conscientious as possible about giving the public what in general is considered to be good taste or good design. I thought it was such an opportunity, and it worked very well, that's all I can say.[56]

RICHARD GUMP'S AXIOMS OF GOOD TASTE

1. Age is not an automatic measure of value.
2. A work of art is a work of art in any material.
3. An out-of-the-ordinary method of manufacture is not a guarantee of extraordinary value.
4. A foreign stamp is no criterion for extra value.
5. Costliness does not necessarily assure comeliness.
6. A master does not always create a masterpiece.
7. The relics of the renowned aren't always desirable.

Left: Looking across at 250 Post Street, designed by architect Clinton Day. Gump's moved into the building in 1909 and stayed there until it relocated in 1995. *OpenSFHistory/ wnp100.00065.jpg.*

Below: Looking west on Post Street toward Union Square in the late '50s; Gump's is on the right with the St. Francis Hotel in the distance. *SFMTA Photo | SFMTA.com/photo.*

8. Over elaboration is not beauty.

9. The latest thing is not the best thing per se.

10. It is crazy to try to live beyond your means—financially, culturally or physically.

11. Emotional reactions, personal prejudices and predilections do not point the way; to reach the right destination it is necessary to understand and appreciate the basics of good design.

12. There are worthwhile things and many worthless things on the market.[57]

Gump's was strict about whom it hired; Richard didn't like people who worked in merchandising who had poor taste and big reputations. After he published his book *Good Taste Costs No More* in 1951, he decided that all current employees and applicants would take his 137-question Design Test. However, Marilu Klar, who ended up working at Gump's for more than fifty years and was the official curator of pearls and gemstones, refused to take it when she was interviewed. She told Richard that she already knew she had good taste, so why should she take the test? He still hired her. As Richard said in his oral history:

I picked out about 200 pictures of all kinds of things, rooms, objects, old and modern. When I say "modern" I mean modern design, no period influence.... And the test subjects are supposed to select and to say whether they're good or bad. I never found anybody with good taste who did badly on the test or anybody with poor taste who did well on it....I wanted somebody who had a feel for merchandising as well as a feel for the use of things.[58]

For fifty years, until her retirement in 1972, Eleanor Forbes (always known as "Miss Forbes") helped define "good taste" at Gump's and was the driving force behind Gump's Design Studio (the term "interior decorating" was retired). Custom interiors, furniture design, fabric design, glassware, china, pottery and jewelry—Miss Forbes and her staff were known for their elegant simplicity and could do it all. She became very well known as a designer and eventually worked for other designers such as John and Elinor McGuire of McGuire Furniture. Paul Faria, who managed the department in the late '50s, with Miss Forbes as lead designer, said in an interview:

Before we put a design on the floor, we knew what the customer was going to buy. It practically never failed....Of course, all good buyers know what their customers want. Except in our case we started from scratch. We'd

Good taste and good design were at the foundation of Gump's merchandising. It served the store well for over one hundred years. *Author's collection.*

design it and put it together....If you have something—say a table that is going to cost $600—you know the customer won't buy it at that price, so you won't make it. You'd say, "I'm going to make a table that looks like that and it's got to sell for $325." Otherwise you're a bad merchandiser....We had an edge....We were the manufacturer so we did not have to take just what was available.[59]

And so the store thrived, consistently innovating to present creative wares to a loyal customer base with pent-up demand let loose after the war years. From its gallery to its jade trees to its Christmas windows, Gump's set the bar high.

The Gump's Gallery, for example, showcased historical and contemporary paintings, prints, sculpture and American crafts, carrying major artists such as Motherwell, de Kooning, Picasso, Oliveira, Calder and Rauschenberg. Crafts artists included Gilhooly and William Morris. The Gump's Gallery displays were notable enough that the records are preserved in the Smithsonian's Archives of American Art. (Some didn't think so highly of it. Gump's was the "Metropolitan Museum with cash registers," according to colorful local Sally Stanford—a madam, restaurateur and mayor of Sausalito, briefly married to Robert Gump.)[60]

The Gump's windows were art pieces as well. After Richard became manager, he worked with a talented display director, Don Smith, on a new visual system that discarded what he called the "supermarket apple pyramid school." Their thinking was that windows are three-dimensional spaces, so why not have the merchandise become part of the design? Take a set of dinnerware and put the five basic parts on the floor, but have other serving pieces dangling by invisible wires in the space. The department heads weren't happy at first, but then sales increased and that was that.

Gump's Christmas windows were worth a trip downtown. Eight glass-enclosed chambers faced Post Street and were a big draw every Christmas. In the '80s, a staff of six worked for six months (at an estimated cost of $100,000) to create scenes with falling snow and Japanese dolls. There was a bit of a crisis when the plastic snow was sticking to the glass, but a resourceful employee came up with the idea of spraying the snow with a static preventer, and that solved the problem.

And starting in 1987, the biggest hit of all was when the windows featured adoptable animals from the SPCA. One year there were miniature rooms in a Victorian mansion, with cats on small, elegantly upholstered armchairs. Puppies frolicked in living rooms with tiny grandfather clocks. Best of all, each season about 250 kittens and puppies found new homes.

Even Gump's gift wrapping department was distinctive. If you ask locals, they say "Billy" was the best of Gump's many talented wrappers. The understated Gump's logo was discreetly displayed on a gold box with red ribbon. Bernadette Hooper, who worked at Gump's from late 1978 to 1993, says that when the United Nations charter was signed in San Francisco in 1945, it was entrusted to the Gump's wrapping department to package it carefully to send east.

DEDICATED, KNOWLEDGEABLE SALES FORCE

Many former employees speak admiringly of their experience. Said Paul Faria, who managed the design department under Richard Gump:

> *When you have employees at all levels enthusiastically contributing to the overall planning, you stimulate creativity and high morale. To me that was one of the strengths of the store, that everybody was involved in it, like a big family….And Mr. Gump at the end of the year would say, "We've had a wonderful year. Please do it again next year." He didn't pressure you day by day; he just wanted that by the end of the year you'd had a good year.*[61]

San Franciscan Denise Pereira Webster, who started working during the Christmas season at Gump's in 1970 when she was a student, says it was her first exposure to beautiful things; she bought her first china set while working at the store. "Most college students go on ski trips, but I had a full set of china. That's where I spent my money." Webster says Gump's was very generous to her. She started as a gift wrapper and was soon working in the jewelry department: "I was able to live in two worlds—as a college student, paying my way through, and at Gump's, where I would wear $35,000 necklaces. We had to put on the jewelry to display and we had to wear black—it either had to have a split neck or a V-neck so people could see the jewelry on us. I learned a lot about design and the history behind the jewelry."

Gump's wanted to keep her as an employee, even when she told them she wanted to go to UC Berkeley full time. They agreed that if she could work two days a week, she could keep her job. That paid her way through college.

Besides wearing fabulous jewelry (that tradition was stopped after someone stole a $50,000 necklace), Webster came in contact with a lot of celebrities. She waited on Jack Lemmon and Walter Matthau and their wives. Former mayor Willie Brown would come in with clothier Wilkes Bashford, as did actor Robert Wagner ("probably the handsomest man I had ever seen in my life at that point"). The "Spreckels ladies," two descendants of Alma de Bretteville Spreckels and sugar magnate Adolph Spreckels, would make weekly visits. "All the rich ladies would regularly come to the store," recalls Webster. "They would buy things for the opera opening, or this opening or this show or event. Since I was the young girl, I wasn't allowed to wait on them—only the seasoned pros could. My job was to stand there with a cup of tea and hold it for one of them."

Webster, who worked at the store until the mid-'70s, says the experience made a big impression on her: "It changed my life, and will always have a special place in my heart. It was where I really felt like a San Franciscan."

Bernadette Hooper, who worked at Gump's for fourteen-plus years as an assistant credit manager, says:

> *Many of the older sales people in the '70s and '80s were veterans of venerable institutions like the White House and Dohrmann's. I was blown away by their depth of knowledge and how they knew their customers. In all the departments there were experts.*
>
> *Generations returned to the salespeople who had set up their bridal registries when their own children got engaged. I was particularly fond of the staff of the Silver Department (Virginia Fields, Meg Rouda,*

Ruth Geary, Allen Nissim, Becky Wallace, Paul Price, etc.). Mrs. Fields remembered customers' silver patterns decades after their weddings. ("Your pattern is on sale. Would you like to order the last four butter knives?")

Sales staff knew who to go to for that "extra bit" of information. One day I was with the assistant controller, Wilson Chan, when Bill Wilson from Asian Antiques made a request. A couple from Scotland had just purchased a Chinese scroll and wanted a translation. Could Mr. Chan assist? Indeed he could. ("The river rises in the spring and flows down the mountain…") Bill left Mr. Chan's office beaming.

Hooper also recalls that in the '70s, copies of all store correspondence were kept in a file room next to the cashier's office. Chris Stritzinger "Stritz," chairman of the store's board, could often be found there reading random letters for quality control. If a letter didn't meet his standards for clear communication, correct spelling, punctuation, etc., the writer would receive a "marked" copy, courtesy of the board chair.

SO WHAT HAPPENED?

In 1969, Richard Gump sold the store for an estimated $12 million to Crowell Collier and Macmillan Inc. and agreed to lead it for another five years. He was sixty-three years old, and there wasn't another Gump generation to take it over. Richard had a son, Peter, from one of his marriages, but Peter wasn't involved with the store. One newspaper said the sale was a move to lessen future inheritance taxes.[62] In a note to employees on the day of his retirement, Richard noted that Macmillan would continue "our famed merchandising tradition developed over a century and based on quality, knowledge, imagination and good taste."[63]

Richard's longtime assistant, Clariece Graham, to whom he left part of the proceeds from the sale of his art collection after his death in 1989, said, "He went by instinct. He felt that if it was the right thing to do, it was the right thing to do.…In my opinion, Mr. Gump's retirement from the store left a void in San Francisco's arts and antiques circle, and it will never be the same."[64]

Even without a Gump at the helm, the store survived under a revolving door of owners for almost fifty more years, until the fall of 2018, when it declared bankruptcy, liquidated its stock and closed its doors in late

In 1949, in honor of his father and brothers, Richard Gump donated an eleven-foot-high, one-and-a-half-ton bronze Buddha to the Japanese Tea Garden in Golden Gate Park. *Philippe Teuwen.*

December 2018. Macmillan owned it for two decades, opening stores in Beverly Hills, Houston and Dallas in the early '80s. When Robert Maxwell, the flamboyant British media mogul, took over Macmillan, the company decided Gump's did not fit with its longtime core publishing business. In 1989, Macmillan sold it for more than $35 million to a group consisting of Charterhouse Equity Partners and Tobu Department Stores of Japan. The Houston and Dallas stores closed in early 1991 and Beverly Hills in 1992.

In 1993, Hanover Direct (formerly Horn & Hardart) purchased the store and its mail-order operation in Texas for about $13 million and worked on building its e-commerce and catalogue business. In late 1994, rumors swirled as the company basically lost its lease at 250 Post Street amid infighting between the banks and family trusts that owned the building. In 1995, under the watchful eye of New York retailing executive Geraldine Stutz, who headed Henri Bendel from 1958 to 1985, the store relocated with great fanfare one and a half blocks east to 135 Post Street. A large bronze Buddha presided over the seventeen thousand square feet of retail space, and Stutz

The twenty-first-century Gump's offered a wide range of china patterns, with designs aimed to appeal to both traditional tastes and more eclectic. *Torbakhopper.*

In 1995, Gump's moved to 135 Post Street, its last location. It had been located at 250 Post since after the 1906 earthquake and fire. *Author's collection.*

sought to strengthen the store's image, aiming for a young, contemporary, value-oriented clientele.

However, Hanover struggled and ended up selling the business to three private equity firms in 2005 for $8.5 million. Under Hanover's ownership, the catalogue and website had offered different items than the store. The new owners invested heavily in aligning all the sales channels and increased the catalogue mailings from ten million to twelve million.

The business held on for another 13 years, finally succumbing after 157 years. It was not a question of expanding too fast, as, unlike I. Magnin, it chose to open only a few branch stores, which had closed almost three decades earlier. The brand had made a valiant effort to capture the growth of e-commerce; at the time of the closing, purchases on its website and catalogue accounted for more than 75 percent of sales. The Gump's name may not be gone forever, though, as it was announced in late June 2019 that the family of John Chachas, founder and managing principal of Methuselah Advisors, a New York investment bank, had bought Gump's brand and trademarks and plans to run an online business and open at least a temporary store in San Francisco. Chachas, previously a Gump's board member and investor, is reluctant to commit to a permanent store because of the state of San Francisco streets, which he considers unhealthy for luxury retail.[65] Time will tell whether the store can make a comeback.

If not, then goodbye to the temple of good taste, the goddesses, the pearls, the bowls of jade flowers, the custom stationery, the Baccarat and Steuben crystal, the myriad patterns of fine china, crystal and silver flatware. The original Buddha won't be back, as Chachas, the new owner, auctioned it at Christie's in Hong Kong in late May 2019; it fetched about $4 million. A.L. Gump would have been proud.

Chapter 4

I. MAGNIN & CO., 1876–1994

"Magninique!"

WHO WAS THE "I. MAGNIN WOMAN"?

She was a woman who trusted I. Magnin to choose items of the highest quality, whether it was a bottle of perfume or a dress. She was a dedicated customer who, after her initial visit, would often just call her salesperson to order. "Her" salesperson would keep notes in her "Bluebook" of all her clients' preferences. The I. Magnin woman might have a trust fund that only paid out once a year, so she would charge everything at I. Magnin, and the store would wait to be paid until her annual check came in. She might need a new lipstick and would call in her order. Her driver would pull up at the door, and the I. Magnin doorman would hand her driver the package. If she wore custom couture, then she turned to Henriette de Clert (Madame Moon) or Stella Hanania (Miss Stella) to be her private buyers, as they combed the European collections for their clientele in San Francisco and Southern California, returning to create top-of-the-line elegant outfits. Her furs were stored in I. Magnin's fur vault, keeping them safe until the next opera or ballet opening. She lunched and watched the fashion show from one of the best seats on Mondays in the Mural Room at the St. Francis Hotel, dressed in her best suit, hat and gloves—from I. Magnin, of course. A *Vogue* magazine article describes the idealized I. Magnin ambiance:

> *Fur jackets suggest a mink or two in the cupboard and a place in the country. Tiny lace pillows…sketch out mornings in bed with an immaculate breakfast tray brought in by an adoring maid. Never mind that these things may be*

Who could resist the fresh flowers from the friendly vendors outside I. Magnin and around Union Square? *Fred Lyon.*

totally absent from the reality of one's life....By shopping in a place where everything is reputed to be both the best and the finest, we are buying a taste that we may not have been born with....I. Magnin...promises a perfect life.[66]

Yet I. Magnin had more shoppers than just Pacific Heights matrons. An aspiring I. Magnin customer, a girl in her teens, might have her first bra fitted by Mrs. Swallow. Or she might venture to the third-floor gown salon to

Left: The ten-floor I. Magnin store in 1955, with its exterior of white Vermont marble, viewed from Union Square. *San Francisco History Center, San Francisco Public Library.*

Right: The I. Magnin woman could depend on the store to find her the perfect gown for the opera or symphony openings. *Author's collection.*

find a special dress for a prom or black-tie dance. Saleswomen would coolly assess her as she exited the elevator and politely suggest she try the sixth floor instead, where the junior Marima department was. It would take a courageous teen to persevere and tell the third-floor saleswoman that no, she wanted one of their gowns on the third floor. The saleswomen, after their initial suggestion to try an alternate department, would take care of her and find that perfect dress, whether it was on the third floor or the sixth. After that shopping adventure, one could always go rest in the fifth-floor restroom and powder room, a downtown oasis famous for its green marble, gilt ceiling and Art Deco pedestal sinks.

How did this West Coast institution get its start, rise to become a thirty-one-store chain in 1990 with dedicated customers throughout the West and then lose its touch and its many loyal customers? By 1994, the I. Magnin logo on the "marble palace" on Union Square was no more, and Macy's took over the building.

MARY ANN MAGNIN—A RETAIL POWERHOUSE IN A SMALL PACKAGE

I. Magnin and Co.'s roots were very deep in San Francisco, starting with Mary Ann and Isaac Magnin, who immigrated to the Bay Area in the mid-1870s. Born in Scheveningen, Holland, in 1849, Mary Ann Cohen met Isaac Magnin, who had also been born in Holland and was a wood carver and gilder, in London. Isaac had come to the United States from England before the Civil War when he was fifteen, unwillingly served in the army (whether it was for the Union or Confederate is unclear, as sources vary) and was wounded. After a stint as a pushcart peddler in New Orleans, Isaac returned to England, where he met and married Mary Ann (who was in her mid-teens) in 1865.

After they married, Isaac wanted to return to the United States, but Mary Ann did not want to leave while her mother was still alive. When Mary Ann's mother passed, she and Isaac and their seven children (Samuel, Henrietta, Joseph, Emanuel John, Victor, Lucille and Flora) immigrated to San Francisco, coming via ship around Cape Horn in 1875. Their youngest child, Grover, was born in San Francisco in 1885.

Mary Ann, the "real" founder of I. Magnin & Company, began her retail career when she and Isaac (the *I* in I. Magnin) first opened a tiny neighborhood store in Oakland. They then moved to San Francisco and opened a store south of Market Street in 1876, selling notions: pins, needles, thread, buttons and tobacco. An expert seamstress, Mary Ann also plied her needle making layettes, delicate lingerie and shirtwaists.

Mary Ann Magnin, the powerhouse behind I. Magnin in the early days. *San Francisco History Center, San Francisco Public Library.*

Although Isaac was an excellent gilder by profession, working for S. & G. Gump when he first arrived in San Francisco, he was a dreamer and student by choice. Says their great-granddaughter Ellen Magnin Newman, "We called her 'Queen Victoria' and her husband 'Karl Marx.' Isaac, after whom the store was named, was a frame builder and very much a Communist. He would be at Union Square, revolutionizing the world." A 1936 *Time* magazine article described Isaac as "a linguist and amateur philosopher who quoted continually from Edward Bellamy (Looking Backward), he [Isaac Magnin] used to pedal his bicycle around and around Golden Gate Park, pockets crammed with Marxian tracts and pamphlets."[67]

According to I. Magnin lore, Mary Ann Magnin was a tireless worker, rising at dawn to be at wholesalers to buy her materials, scouting out the finest. She would sell her goods during the day and, in the evening, supervise the cutting of garments for the next day's work. And this was in addition to caring for her large brood of children.

Isaac Magnin, Mary Ann's husband, worked as an expert gilder but preferred reading and distributing political tracts. *San Francisco History Center, San Francisco Public Library.*

In an oft-repeated story about Mary Ann and Isaac, Solomon Gump, Isaac's employer, offered him a promotion and extra pay if he would decorate the ceiling of a church that had a lot of gold leaf, which was Isaac's specialty. Isaac was delighted about the prospect, but Mary Ann was less than thrilled. According to her son Grover, she said:

"You are not going to take the job, you never worked on a scaffold and you will fall down and break your neck." Father replied, "We have eight people to feed including you and me, they have to eat," and Mother responded, "I'll show you how they'll eat." She was very handy with a needle and started making baby clothes and sold them from her home.[68]

Word spread quickly about Mary Ann's exquisite needlework, and soon the store stopped carrying notions and focused on lingerie, shirtwaists and infants' wear. Bridal trousseaus and baby layettes were a specialty, and the society ladies of San Francisco—Nob Hill matrons who were the new nobility, the wives of mining kings, lumber barons and railroad czars—took notice. Mary Ann's high-quality goods were popular not only with the ladies of Nob Hill, but the demimonde of the Barbary Coast also appreciated her beautiful lingerie. As the business prospered, Mary Ann took on helpers and moved to larger quarters.

FOCUS ON QUALITY

To Mary Ann, quality was everything. As her son Grover, who was president of the store from 1944 to 1951, said, "One thing I learned early in business—that nothing was forgotten as quickly as price if you backed it up with the right quality and style."[69] To teach Grover about quality, according to Grover's wife, Jeanne Magnin, Mary Ann would blindfold him and then have him touch handmade lace and silk and fine damask to learn to identify them by feel.[70]

Conversation around the dinner table was usually about the store, and Mary Ann instilled in her children the fundamental practices of running a successful business. The boys helped out from an early age, making deliveries, sweeping the store, working in the stockroom and running errands. The girls were expected to learn needlework and marry into respectable families, which they did. "She would lecture her children by the hour about buying only the best, but she herself was very frugal. She was, in short, a penny-pinching, stubborn woman who never bought unwisely."[71]

In 1892, Mary Ann decided her son Emmanuel John (John) would take over the business, and he did, at the tender age of twenty-one, bypassing his older brothers Joseph and Samuel. One article said that Mary Ann had consulted a palmist, who advised her to choose John.[72] Joseph, who felt he would never rise in the ranks of I. Magnin, would leave the family fold in 1913 to found Joseph Magnin, a retail powerhouse in its own right. In 1900, Mary Ann retired from the day-to-day operations but definitely kept an eye on things with daily visits to the Union Square store.

After Isaac's death in 1907, Mary Ann lived at the St. Francis Hotel on Union Square (as did her son Grover and his wife, Jeanne) and, in her later years, had her Cadillac retrofitted so it would fit her wheelchair. Her daily routine included a drive down the San Francisco Peninsula in her limousine, lunch at a Burlingame restaurant, a visit to the main store and then dinner in the hotel's dining room. Diminutive, dynamic, single-minded and bossy, Mary Ann also played a mean game of poker, inviting I. Magnin male department heads for Saturday night games. They knew better than to refuse and that it might be best if she won. Mary Ann finally slowed down, passing away at ninety-five in her hotel suite in 1943. No longer would the hotel host an annual birthday party, where some fifty of her children, grandkids and other relatives would gather around to celebrate.

MOVING UP—BECOMING A RETAIL JUGGERNAUT

In those early years before the 1906 earthquake, the store would relocate as its growth required. From its initial location on 5th Street, south of Market Street in San Francisco, it moved to 3rd Street in 1878 and then to Market Street, a busy thoroughfare, in the late 1880s. Business continued to expand, and after relocating several times on Market Street, in 1905, I. Magnin & Co. began to construct a six-story building at Grant Avenue and Geary Boulevard, a very fashionable shopping district. That same year, John Magnin ("Mr. John" to the employees) moved to New York and established a New York buying office. Some said it was to get out from under his mother's iron rule, but the company took the position that to be in daily touch with the style creators in America and Europe, New York was the place to be. John Magnin became a permanent resident, living at the Hotel Savoy-Plaza and spending three months a year in Europe. Grover, the youngest Magnin and Mary Ann's favorite son, was groomed to become the general manager.

In April 1906, the earthquake leveled the I. Magnin store that was under construction. Resourceful Mary Ann responded by setting up shop in her

I. Magnin's temporary home after the earthquake was at Van Ness Avenue at Bush Street, the fringe of the fire line. *California History Room, California State Library, Sacramento, California.*

family home at Page and Masonic Streets. The butler's pantry was the packing room, three bedrooms were used for fitting rooms and the dining room was the blouse department. They placed ads in the newspapers requesting that employees return to work at the Magnins' home. John and Grover were able to get new stock into the city from a customshouse in Oakland, and customers flocked to the temporary store in hacks (horse-drawn vehicles), as streetcars were not running.

By July, they had moved to a temporary store on Van Ness Avenue at Bush Street, the fringe of the fire line, where other stores had set up temporary headquarters while they rebuilt. Getting an insurance payout was an issue since many of the insurance companies had defaulted, so I.W. Hellman, president of Wells Fargo Bank, gave John Magnin a loan of $50,000, without security, to construct the temporary building on Van Ness.

By 1909, a new four-story store designed by the Chicago architect Louis Taussig had opened on Grant Avenue with three floors of selling space and a floor for alterations and workrooms. By this time, there was a move away from made-to-measure tailored suits and dresses, and the new store offered a full line of ready-to-wear clothing and millinery. As a *San Francisco Chronicle* article described the opening:

> *Store is thronged: From the minute the doors of the great establishment were opened last evening, a constant stream of visitors thronged the store, filling the aisles and the spacious floors. They came trooping along in almost endless number, on foot, in carriages and automobiles....Every floor is stocked with the choicest articles of woman's and infants' wear, made of the finest fabrics and in the latest fashion, culled from the best sources.*[73]

Twenty-four-year-old Grover Magnin took on the role of manager, and the store was poised to become the West Coast's premier specialty store.

GROVER MAGNIN: QUALITY IS #1

I was the youngest in the family, and by that time [1906], Mother had retired from the business and turned it over to my brother John Magnin to manage; he happened to be the most capable one of the family. He put me through a very severe training and between my Mother and him I had a tight rope to walk....I...learn[ed] every angle of the business meticulously.[74]

Left: Hats, of course, were an essential accessory to complete an ensemble. Your cloche, fascinator or pillbox fit perfectly in your I. Magnin box. *Ron Ross.*

Opposite: Models admire the mink skins and tiny lights hanging on a fourteen-foot Christmas tree on the first floor of I. Magnin's in the early '50s. *San Francisco History Center, San Francisco Public Library.*

Mary Ann liked to keep her brood close by, and in 1913, Grover moved into his own suite, an oak-paneled, two-story apartment at the St. Francis Hotel, right next to his mother. Supposedly there was an unlocked door between their apartments so that Mary Ann could freely visit. That tradition stopped when Grover married Jeanne Melton in 1931. Grover and Jeanne continued to live at the St. Francis for almost forty years (Grover died in 1969), among their collection of Impressionist paintings by such renowned artists as Van Gogh, Pissarro, Renoir and Degas.

Grover carried on Mary Ann's obsession with quality. Even during the Depression, when sales dropped dramatically (from $11 million in 1929 to $5.5 million in 1933), the store did not scrimp on quality. As Miss Elizabeth Curtis, a forty-year employee who was in charge of a dress department at the San Francisco store, said in 1976:

> *Every so often, Mr. Grover would call his top people together and give a little class in quality detection. He'd spread out a handful of different grade pearl necklaces, turn the price tags face down and show us how to select the best. The same thing was done with alligator skins, fur pelts, even samples of tortoise shell. He also told us where the products came from, their romance, their history. It didn't matter what department you were in, these were things he wanted all of us to know. He'd say, "When you sell a*

customer a thirty-five-hundred-dollar Balenciaga or Dior, she has the right to expect reliable counsel on the accessories to go with it.[75]

Another one of Grover's philosophies was his belief that the customer was always right. He established a rule that almost anyone could say yes to a customer, but he reserved the right to be the only one to say no. One day a committee of buyers tried to get him to change the liberal return policy because they believed some customers were taking advantage of it. Grover decided to do some research and asked his accountant to investigate. This accountant was to go through three thousand accounts looking for customers who returned more than 15 percent of their purchases, the percentage that was considered unprofitable. It turned out that less than 5 percent of the I. Magnin customers returned around 15 percent of their purchases. The buyers agreed that penalizing the other 95 percent did not make sense, and that was that.

BRANCHING OUT

From 1912 on, I. Magnin opened small branches along the West Coast, starting with a shop in Santa Barbara in the Potter Hotel. It was initially conceived as what we would call a "pop-up" shop today, built to raise awareness of the brand, but it was such a success that it became a permanent shop. Over the next few years, others opened in resort hotels in Coronado (Hotel del Coronado) and Pasadena (Huntington Hotel). These were the forerunners of branch shops soon to be located from Seattle to La Jolla. Said Eddie Joseph, vice president in 1959:

> *In those magnificent hotels, the thing was to change your clothes five or six times a day and make a grand entrance into the dining room, dressed to the teeth and of course, sit on the porch dressed up. They tell me we sold some of the most fabulous merchandise in those hotel shops at prices for blouses and other handmade things that I'm sure we haven't even come close to in the last 20 years.*[76]

Soon, I. Magnin had freestanding stores dotting the West Coast. Mr. Grover had grand plans for the Los Angeles store, and in 1938, Grover and his architect, Timothy Pflueger, sailed on the *Queen Mary* from New York to Europe in search of fixtures and inspiration for his stores. It was San Francisco–born Pflueger's first trip to Europe, and it was first class all the way, Grover Magnin's usual mode of travel. Pflueger and Magnin were in search of chandeliers for the stores, and after realizing they couldn't find what they wanted locally and in New York, they decided to try to find them in Europe, as Grover recalled in his (unpublished) memoir:

> So we started off and went to New York first and could find nothing there. We got on the old Queen Mary and went to Paris where we couldn't find anything, likewise in London, Venice, Milan, and we did find one chandelier at Lalique in Paris, which was for the center motif of the first floor and we liked it enormously, but they could not make delivery on time, and naturally, we couldn't hold up the opening for the chandelier. Both Tim and myself remembered enough about it and we went to Los Angeles and found the man who could make it for us. Here we had someone in our own backyard. We could have saved time and expense by not going to Europe if we had consulted with this man.[77]

For the new Los Angeles store, to make sure they didn't make any mistakes, Grover built a model of the building (one-quarter size) in white plaster showing all the details. As he said, "This cost $15 or $20 thousand, but what would that be compared to the cost of the building, which would have been about $1.5 million, and then we had made a mistake?"[78]

The Los Angeles store on Wilshire Boulevard, designed by Myron Hunt and H.C. Chambers, with interiors by Timothy Pflueger, opened in February 1939, consolidating three smaller shops that had been in hotels. It was a stunning white marble building with a motor entrance and air conditioning and established the style for subsequent I. Magnin stores.

JOINING FORCES FOR EVEN MORE GROWTH

To continue to grow, it takes cash, and I. Magnin found a suitable partner in Bullock's, a department store chain headquartered in Los Angeles. Bullock's and I. Magnin merged in 1944, combining I. Magnin's eight Pacific coast stores with Bullock's four Southland stores. The two companies combined had a volume of over $60 million in 1943, so this merger created an even stronger retail merchandising operation.

Grover Magnin remained president of I. Magnin & Co., and the entities maintained their distinct identities.[79]

After World War II, under the discerning eye of "Mr. Grover," stores opened all over California and other western states. To name just a few of the locations in California: Sacramento, La Jolla, Fresno, Palo Alto, Santa Ana, Carmel, San Fernando Valley, Santa Clara, San Mateo and Walnut Creek. There were also stores in Portland, Oregon; Phoenix, Arizona; and Chicago, Illinois.

Just as Grover aimed to have the best-dressed clientele, he also personally saw to it that the interior of his stores would be as exciting as the merchandise he was offering. His stores had spacious selling areas with settees or loveseats where customers could sit while saleswomen would bring selections from a stockroom (no racks of clothing cluttering up the sales floor). If a customer wanted to try something on, then it was off to the elegant fitting rooms (with enough space for a friend, a hardy soul who might want to accompany an I. Magnin woman on her shopping trip). Grover was involved in all aspects, from designing the crystal light fixtures and choosing the carpets to selecting the imported marble for the walls. As a company document described it:

> *All are outstanding examples of classic modern architecture—simple façade with vertical lines, some in white marble accented by polished black granite. The interiors are designed to combine luxury with a feeling of intimacy and feminine charm. Walls of Rose de Brignolles marble, high silvered ceilings with bas relief motifs and great chandeliers distinguish the street floors of the Los Angeles, Beverly Hills and San Francisco stores. The display cases are of gold bronze with exquisitely decorated glass panels. The apparel floors are decorated in soft pastel tones, pale wood furniture and delicate fabrics—perfect backgrounds for luxurious I. Magnin fashions.[80]*

By the '40s, it was time for a new flagship store in San Francisco, and Grover had his eye on the ten-story Butler Building at Stockton Street and Geary Boulevard, on Union Square. He and Timothy Pflueger got to work. They stripped the building down to its steel frame and then added a smooth Vermont marble exterior. Grover hated pigeons and made sure the new building façade would not be a welcome place for the birds:

> *"When I hired architect Tim Pflueger to build this store," he* [Grover Magnin] *reminisced, "I told him to make it pigeon-proof. It was the first*

On Geary Boulevard in 1945, the B-line streetcar passes the Butler Building, which is soon to be the home of I. Magnin & Co. *OpenSFHistory/wnp14.3413.jpg.*

thing I thought of, because I live at the St. Francis and I could see what the birds had done to that building. So Magnin's has no ledges or cornices where a pigeon can get a toe-hold."[81]

The first floor had walls of Rose de Brignolles marble from France, five glass murals by Max Ingrand, a molded silver-leaf ceiling and a floor of pink Tennessee marble. Showcases framed in bronze with decorative glass displayed the luxury goods. The eight elevators took customers to the salons on various floors. On the second floor, one could try on evening slippers in a semi-private alcove off the Shoe Room, which was decorated in top-grain eggshell cowhide with bronze trim. On the same floor was the Oval Room for custom millinery, with extruded bronze and Botticino marble trim and mirrored walls (indirectly lighted for a more flattering look). Rounding out the facilities on the second floor: the Negligee and Boudoir Apparel Room. Every floor (except for floors eight to ten, which were for workrooms, executives, employees and the telephone switchboard) had its salon: the Baroque Room, the Fur Room, the Custom Room and, of course, the Powder Room on the fifth floor (a favorite stop for downtown shoppers for many years).

Above: The distinctive interior of the San Francisco store's street floor aimed to combine luxury and a feeling of intimacy. *San Francisco History Center, San Francisco Public Library.*

Left: Beauty consultants gave customers personalized attention at the Powder Bar, in the Charles of the Ritz Beauty Salon Reception Room. *San Francisco History Center, San Francisco Public Library.*

It's not many retail bathrooms that inspire Facebook posts. Magnin's bathroom, with its Art Deco pedestal sinks with gold faucets, dark green marble walls, Italian mirrors and gilt ceiling, is cited in many nostalgic Facebook entries and was still accessible until the building's 2019 sale. The lovely powder room, a "marble oasis," was even a finalist in Cintas Corp.'s annual "America's Best Public Restroom" contest in 2009.

When I. Magnin opened the new store in 1948…we were all so proud. Thanks to the genius of the late architect, Timothy Pflueger, the building was, and is still, the most beautiful in town….Due to World War II, there was still a steel shortage so I. Magnin went up around the steel skeleton of the old Butler office building…The interior was dazzling, especially the great main hall, two stories high, with its Lalique light fixtures, the gold ceilings, the glass murals, the expensively made cases. "Price was no object,"

Customers could sit in an elegant showroom while saleswomen brought selections from a stockroom (no racks of clothing cluttered up the sales floor). *San Francisco History Center, San Francisco Public Library.*

The fifth-floor Art Deco bathroom was famous for pedestal sinks with gold faucets, dark green marble walls, Italian mirrors and gilt ceiling. *San Francisco History Center, San Francisco Public Library.*

beamed Grover Magnin. "Of course, a dress will cost a little more but isn't it all great fun?" Christian Dior came from Paris to utter "Magnifique!" "There's our new slogan," announced Grover. "Magninique."[82]

Unfortunately, Timothy Pflueger did not live to see the completed store, which opened in 1948. After his usual evening swim at the Olympic Club on November 20, 1946, he died suddenly of a heart attack at the age of fifty-four. This largely self-taught architect who never was educated beyond high school and was one of seven sons raised in the Mission district left the Bay Area richer than he found it. In addition to the I. Magnin flagship store, he designed landmarks such as the 450 Sutter Street building, the Castro and Paramount theaters and the Pacific Telephone Building, a skyscraper when it was finished in 1927 and the tallest building in the city.

THE MAGNIN EMPLOYEE—FORGING RELATIONSHIPS KEY

"It was the most magical thing I've ever experienced in and out of a store. Every day I couldn't wait to get there," says Richard Bayne, who came from a career in retail in New York and worked at Magnin's from 1984 to 1994, mostly in cosmetics and perfume. Former employee Ginnie Miraglia, who worked there in the late '80s and again from 1992 to 1994, agrees: "How do I describe it? I loved getting up to go to work every day. I worked in a lovely environment. It was a beautiful store." Miraglia had also come from New York and had worked at Bloomingdale's. She worked in trend jewelry and then moved to the sixth floor, where she sold apparel. Miraglia liked her Magnin's manager and loved the people and clients. "Our typical customer was from Pacific Heights and Nob Hill, but when they had the ad for the Schrader dresses for $69 in the spring, ladies would come from all over."

Says Bayne, "I was a New Yorker, so I was very aggressive, but I learned quickly that the velvet glove treatment was what the store was all about, so I had to really tone it down." On a typical day, "we would get in the store and an announcement would come over the loudspeaker; they would list the number-one department and what they sold the previous day: 'Richard was number one with $5,000 yesterday, or $12,000…' Then they would continue with store announcements and pep talks: 'Today we're having Nolan Miller from *Dynasty* coming with his couture…' Or Galanos, Oscar De La Renta,

Designer Christian Dior (*center*) in 1955 with Magnin's queen of custom couture, Miss Stella Hanania, on his left and I. Magnin president Hector Escobosa to her left. *San Francisco History Center, San Francisco Public Library.*

Carolina Herrera or Bob Mackie. Every couture designer came through the store to do their personal trunk shows all the time."

Brent McDaneld was with I. Magnin for fifteen years, coming up through the ranks and holding several positions at the company. By 1995, he was executive vice president of communications. He says, "We always strove to be first. The first to feature collections from Christian Dior in the United States, the first to feature collections from a young Yves Saint Laurent, the first to help launch the careers of many designers, including Vera Wang and Isaac Mizrahi. Each year, I. Magnin gave the prestigious Mary Ann

Magnin Fashion Award to a deserving designer at the annual San Francisco Fall Fashion Show benefiting the San Francisco Ballet."

Arthur Corbin, who worked at Magnin's shortly after high school in the late '60s, remembers that the sales ladies were all very well dressed. Rosemary Klebahn, a former buyer, recalled her training days and the instructions on dress: "We had to wear black, navy, grey or brown. We were supposed to disappear, and we were to wear girdles because nothing could shake or jiggle."[83] Corbin remembers, "They had a very strict dress code for employees—I had to wear a tie, even though I was working in the back. My job was to take shoes to the floor."

Richard Bayne says that some of the sales ladies who worked there didn't really need to; they had married well but liked working there to take advantage of the employee discount. "They looked like paintings, all of them. They had the jewelry and Chanel suits and it was mind-boggling."

As you got off the elevator there would be a formidable group of sales ladies who would assess whether you should just be shown some clothes on a hanger, or if you were a better prospect, a model (always size 6) would model the dress.

Bayne recalls, "At Magnin's, they just gave you free rein and once you got a customer, the entire store was at your disposal to inter-sell. So if you had a customer who liked you, you could sell her a fur coat as well as a lipstick. You could go anywhere you wanted to." Employees also had their other favorite go-to employees, says Bayne:

> You'd have your favorite wrapper, or I would give samples to a telephone operator so she would ring my extension. A few years after I started, I was given my own section.…Those little squares where everybody works from are called "bays" in cosmetics. They had one in the very center of the store under the clock and they called that the "beauty spot." And every week it changed product. It was for new launches, new perfumes, specials and gifts with purchases—whatever promotion was going on. For a whole year, I had product launch. The vendors would buy the windows for the week. I had four house models hawking my product, and I was in the center ringing it up like a madman. That was my award-winning year. I sold over $500,000 worth of cosmetics that year, and that was in the '80s. I'm telling you, that was incredible, a special moment.

Magnin's took care of its employees in myriad ways. The flagship building housed a seven-bed hospital and private-duty nurse, an employee cafeteria, a sun deck and a lounge. It offered a profit-sharing program and established the MATE Foundation (Magnin Aid to Employees), another valued benefit. Says former employee Ginnie Miraglia, "They were very generous. I was told that if I needed any money, we will take care of you. I had asked because I thought my brother might need my help." Arthur Corbin had the same experience: "The foundation helped me with my rent when I was in some difficulties, and they didn't expect to get paid back." Corbin added that the foundation also gave scholarships to kids of employees.

Magnin's not only took care of its employees but was also very involved in the community. Brent McDaneld, the former executive vice president, says that I. Magnin didn't just open as many stores as it could in various locations: "We worked diligently to follow the foundation of community involvement that Mary Ann and her sons set. They made it a point to be involved in the local communities where I. Magnin had a store, supporting the Junior League, opera, symphony, ballet, AIDS, breast cancer research and many, many others." In San Francisco, says McDaneld:

> *I. Magnin was the first national department store to host an AIDS benefit when the crisis started. San Franciscans pulled together to raise $250,000 at this fashion event titled "Raise the Roof," held on the roof top of the San Francisco store. For many years I. Magnin also funded and produced the Annual Valentine Ball at the San Francisco Museum of Modern Art. This much-awaited event brought many fashion designers and celebrities throughout the years, including Audrey Hepburn, Sharon Stone and many others.*

FOR THAT VERY SPECIAL CUSTOMER—I. MAGNIN COUTURE

For the I. Magnin woman who could afford it, Madame Moon (Henriette de Clert) was her fashion expert. Madame Moon reigned supreme in the I. Magnin world of couture. Margaret Gault, who moved to San Francisco in the early '50s, used to go to I. Magnin with her friend Lee, an heiress from Seattle. Gault says:

> *Lee dressed beautifully. She bought French couture. To do that, if you lived in Seattle, you would come down to San Francisco to I. Magnin and have an appointment with Madame Moon. Madame Moon was a French woman,*

and as the couture buyer for Magnin's, she went to Paris twice a year and went to all the designers' fashion shows and chose designs that she thought her very wealthy clients would buy, bringing them back to Magnin's. I've always loved clothes and fashion, and even though my circumstances were very different than Lee's, I enjoyed these visits to Madame Moon just as much as my friend did.

When you got off the elevator, Madame Moon was there to greet you. Margaret's friend Lee was able to try on the samples because she was the same size (6!), and if she wanted to buy something, they made a copy of the design for her, at about $5,000 a gown. "Madame Moon was a delightful personality in every way," says Gault. "After we spent a couple of hours looking at the clothes, we took Madame Moon out to lunch. We always went to El Prado in the Hotel Plaza across Union Square. It was a beautiful restaurant."

SO WHAT HAPPENED? THE DOWAGER EMPRESS BEGINS TO STUMBLE

It's a familiar story: decades of growth and expansion and then, with an eye to even more growth, a sale to a bigger entity, and then within a decade or two yet another sale. Times change and shopping patterns change. The "I. Magnin Woman," with her designer clothes and discreet strand of pearls, was no longer relevant as more and more women joined the workforce in the '70s and had less time and interest in couture and rare perfume and the luxury shopping experience.

"Mr. Grover" retired at the mandatory age of sixty-five in 1951, and merchandising whiz Hector Escobosa became president until his sudden death from a heart attack in 1963. After that, a series of executives took the helm and worked to keep ahead of the stiff competition such as Saks Fifth Avenue, Nordstrom and Neiman Marcus. I. Magnin was slow putting self-service racks on the floors (remember those daunting saleswomen one encountered when exiting the elevator?). Ten-dollar "gold" necklaces were displayed next to the real thing. Polyester and knit clothing were available in the moderate lines (Mary Ann Magnin would have been appalled). In the mid-'60s, they brought in a new executive, Catherine Wueste, to cater to the under-twenty-five market. Wueste, described as a "go-go-know-know,"

Looking east down Geary with the B-line streetcar passing by the City of Paris, I. Magnin and Blum's. *OpenSFHistory/wnp32.2418.jpg.*

responsible for such departments as the Ranleigh, Marima and I. Magnin-Hi, left after eighteen months.

The news media seemed to focus on I. Magnin being unable to lure the younger customer, which Brent McDaneld disagrees with: "We had a good number of younger consumers." However, *Women's Wear Daily*, in an article comparing I. Magnin, the dowager empress, to J. Magnin, the kicky upstart, said:

> *It is not clear whether IMCO (I. Magnin & Co.), for reasons of its own, chose merely to nip at the heels of the youth market while competitors were beginning to chew voraciously, or whether the old girl really didn't hear the drums....The dowager aunt is trying to toss a swinging party for the kids with Kool Aid and cookies. But she's trying...and the consensus has it that, given a bit more time, she'll dig. No one turns on young overnight.*[84]

Between 1940 and 1990, I. Magnin changed hands several times, and each new parent was unable to truly reverse the downward trend. Looking at the sequence of acquisitions and sales really illustrates the upheavals in the retail industry (which continue to this day). One needs a scoreboard to keep track of all the players. After the merger with Bullock's in 1944,

Federated Department Stores bought the combined Bullock's and I. Magnin in 1964.

One stellar success, however, was the world-famous I. Magnin catalogue. At the height of the '70s and '80s, well before the Internet, it was a $400 million business, incredible for a catalogue in those days, according to McDaneld, who was heavily involved. Rather than scrolling and clicking "Buy," customers called or faxed in their orders.

In 1988, New York–based Macy's purchased the two companies, consisting of the twenty-five I. Magnin stores and twenty-nine Bullock's/ Bullock's Wilshire stores in Southern California. I. Magnin "has not been much of a profit-maker in the last three years, but if we run the business properly, we can correct that," Macy's chairman Edward Finkelstein said in an interview. "It's a 'wonderful franchise,'" said Finkelstein, but he added that the 111-year-old chain needed to improve its profitability. Finkelstein declared that Magnin's would keep its own name and identity and that Macy's wouldn't "bust down any walls" between its Union Square store and the adjacent I. Magnin. Of course, that didn't turn out to be the case.[85]

In 1992, Macy's, having filed for bankruptcy protection, began closing I. Magnin stores, part of its strategy to focus on I. Magnin's more profitable stores, including San Francisco. In July 1994, Federated was back in the picture when Macy's announced its agreement to merge with it and emerged from Chapter 11 protection by early 1995. The final blow came in November 1994, when the newly merged Macy's/Federated decided that continuing operating I. Magnin did not make economic sense. Jerry Magnin, Cyril Magnin's son and great-grandson of founder Mary Ann Magnin, made a last-ditch effort to save the chain by offering $40 million, which Federated rejected, believing it could generate higher proceeds by liquidating inventory and selling sites.

In the end, four I. Magnin stores were converted to Macy's or Bullock's, and all other I. Magnin operations were discontinued in January 1995. A notice went out to fur storage customers to pick up their furs from the fur vault by December 31, 1994. In early 2019, the flagship store on Union Square changed hands again, and Macy's, as part of Macy's real estate liquidations, sold the "white marble lady" to developer Sand Hill Property Co. for $250 million.

The enormity of the loss of I. Magnin, Grover Magnin's white marble palace at Geary and Stockton, is just beginning to sink in. It's doomed, it's closing, the closeout sale is on, "All Sales Final," nice to have known you, *this way out. Nobody who cares enough about San Francisco, or understands it, has been in charge there for a long time, and the decision to close it came from—well, where? People we'll never run into [who] killed I. Magnin. If they lived here, maybe we'd have found out why it's closing, and what could have been done to save this most important corner of the downtown city. All we got was a bunch of half-baked theories from "analysts" and some sound bites about the store "not keeping up with the times" and "its customers got old and died." It was "too upscale" and didn't know how to go downscale. What's this all about? The competing stores—Saks, say, and Neiman-Marcus—are run by geniuses and I. Magnin by idiots? There are a lot of people who could have turned "the marble lady" around, among them Jerry Magnin, who put up $40 million in a vain attempt to rescue the beauty from the faceless ones.*[86]

Chapter 5

EMPORIUM, 1896–1996

"California's Largest, America's Grandest, Store"

I was raised in the Sunset District in the '40s. You can believe me when I say we were not rich. Every year my Mom would take me downtown on the N Judah streetcar to visit the Emporium roof where we viewed the ice show for free. We would then walk to Woolworth's counter for an egg salad sandwich. From there we would walk to the florist Podesta Baldocchi. We would walk in one door and make the loop to the exit door, enjoying the beautiful arrangements and the wonderful smells of Christmas pine. There was no charge for this. Nor was there a charge for us to walk into the White House or the City of Paris to see the beautifully decorated three-story tree. We called this "window shopping." The few purchases we made were in the Bargain Basement of the Emporium.[87]
—*Marilyn Lewis*

Many native San Franciscans have fond memories of the "Big E." It was the place where you shopped for back-to-school clothes (probably in the Bargain Basement), got your first grown-up jacket and, last but definitely not least, rode the big slide or the train on the roof at Christmas. Christmas also always meant a visit with Santa and a photo.

The store's location "south of the slot" on Market Street, away from the elegance of Union Square, helped its image as a store that was aimed at a more middle-class clientele. As Jack London described it in the *Saturday Evening Post*:

> *The Slot was an iron crack that ran along the center of Market Street, and from the Slot arose the burr of the ceaseless, endless cable that was*

hitched at will to the [street]cars it dragged up and down.....North of the Slot were the theaters, hotels and shopping district, the banks and the staid, respectable business houses. South of the Slot were the factories, slums, laundries, machine-shops, boiler-works and the abodes of the working class.[88]

The great thing about the Emporium is that it made you feel good if you were middle class, like most of S.F. used to be. You could go in there and feel you could afford things. You went to Saks and Neiman's [Neiman Marcus] to remind yourself you couldn't. It was a great place for the working class to get nice things. For most of us, we have great memories of the Emporium. I always felt at home there, and not so much at the other places.[89]

—*Jack McLaughlin*

Looking east from the intersection of Powell and Market Streets in the late 1950s. *SFMTA Photo | SFMTA.com/photo.*

HANGING OUT IN THE BASEMENT

What do longtime San Franciscans remember most about the Emporium and its basement? Let's start with the food: molasses chews, mint chews, soft-serve chocolate malts, pulled pork barbecue sandwiches, Swedish Fish candy and fresh pineapple juice from the vending machine. One person liked entering through the Jessie Street entrance because the candy section was there. The escalator down was nearby. As far as departments, you couldn't beat the fabric and notions, linens, appliance and shoe departments, stamp and coin collection booths, watch repair shop, booth for bus tickets, photography studio and bookstore. There were lockers in the basement where you could store things while shopping.

Ask a group of people who grew up in San Francisco ("We Grew Up in San Francisco," Facebook) for their childhood memories about shopping with Mom or Grandma at the Emporium, and the reminiscences[90] (some good and some not so good) pour in:

My mom use to drag me down there to the bra table. She liked cotton bras and she could only find them there. I hated it and would find the largest bra I could and hold it up and ask if that was her size. Ooh…she would be so mad!

—Karen Wortham Combs

I was always fascinated with the little machines used for measuring the fabric.…You would hit the little lever to clip the fabric. Once the transaction was done, the salesperson would put the charge slip, money or Emporium credit card in the pneumatic tube.

—Phyllis Amstein Wrzesniewski

When we got old enough to shop on our own, my Mom would let us use her Emporium charge card, [sending us] *with a note saying it was ok, her signature and a limit. A note and you could shop on someone else's charge card! The good ole days!*

—KaThi Lewis

I remember my mom taking me down there to find those "bargain basement sales" for clothing and such. My favorite (and perhaps somewhat violent) memory was when they were having a sale on flatware and Mom found a style she liked but the challenge then became to find eight *matching place*

During its last decades, the store was known as the "Big E," and its logo graced the store's boxes and bags at its eleven branch stores. *Author's collection.*

settings. The catch was that they'd thrown assorted styles into this large, maybe six-inch-high bin and you had to rake through it to find what you wanted. My Mom handed me this large salad serving fork, showed me how to stab into a section, then pull it towards me so I could sift through the utensils and *other people's hands in order to fulfill her twisted desires. LOL!! If any of you were there and I stabbed you, my heartfelt apologies and I hope you got a tetanus shot.*

—*Tisha Jourdain Nutter*

I was on the "Teen Board," [which had] one girl from each of the high schools in the city. They had an annual teenage fashion show. Lots of fun.... The Emporium was a very important part of our lives!

—*Joan King*

I just remember the irregular Levi's jeans. My Mom bought a few pairs for me because they were cheap. I hated them.

—*Pete Chun*

I remember in the women's shoe department, there was a contest going on promoting Famolare shoes, the roller coaster shoes [with thick, wavy soles].…*You had to dance to get those shoes. My sis was so determined to get them; she danced in front of everyone and got them!*

—*Albert Anicete*

Shopping at the Emporium was a memorable experience, but nothing beats the Christmas memories. Before we take a look at the store's history, let's visit with Santa and his elves.

SANTA'S THE STAR

It didn't feel like Christmas until you went downtown to see Santa at the Emporium. To get there, you could walk; take public transportation like the 38 Geary, the 47 Van Ness, the K Ingleside or the N Judah; or your mom could park her Cadillac at the 5th and Mission, O'Farrell or Sutter Stockton garage.

We lived on Union and Hyde and Mom would drive downtown in her 1964 white Cadillac to park at the 5th and Mission Garage. We would walk across Mission Street, through a back alley, and enter the Emporium. We would pass through the men's shoe department and into the central area of the store, under the rotunda.

—*Sandy Halpin*[91]

William H. Meyer, who began with Ringling-Barnum Circus in 1919, came up with the department store rooftop carnival concept and opened his first rooftop attraction at the Emporium in 1947, followed by a similar event in Stonestown a few years later. It was a big hit.

Santa's arrival at the beginning of the holiday season was always an over-the-top show. As a 2012 *San Francisco Chronicle* article described it, "Santa was a complete rock star.…In terms of crowd size and fervor, it looked like a cross between a World Series victory parade and a visit by the pope. Santa always rode in style, whether it was a horse and carriage in the very early years or the Cable Car 'Santa-Cade' in the '40s and '50s."[92] Parts of Market Street and Powell Street were shut down and packed with tens of thousands of people wanting to see Santa arrive. Every year there was something special

For a generation of San Franciscans, you knew it was Christmas when you visited Santa and the rooftop carnival at the Emporium. *Author's collection.*

A promotion stunt for the Big E's Toyland: a pair of dwarves in spacesuits are welcomed by a "Flying Tigress" from the Flying Tiger Line. *San Francisco History Center, San Francisco Public Library.*

to wow the crowds, from five thousand helium balloons to a baby elephant, miniature horse, ice skating queens and assorted drummers and buglers.

As Jennifer McCandless remembers:

> *My dad, who worked on Montgomery Street, would take the bus home and then schlep several of us kids back downtown for all the treats—viewing the Xmas displays in Emporium windows, watching the ice skaters, waiting in line for Santa. I most remember the anticipation—taking several escalators up to the [Emporium] roof.*[93]

On the roof, of course kids could visit with Santa and his elves (often there were two Santas, separated by a screen). Former San Francisco supervisor Angela Alioto told the *San Francisco Chronicle* in 1995, "When I was a child I thought Santa Claus lived on the roof of the Emporium."[94] In the '50s, Santa sat on a white and gold throne. Two women in holiday costumes brought children to him, and Santa would call each by name. In Santa's Merryland, the carnival rides included a Ferris wheel, merry-go-round and train. At one time, the store even had an indoor ice rink.

In 1968, the carnival's giant two-humped slide, Star Trak Slide, was a big hit. Perched on the roof, it was the highest fun slide in the United States. To get installed on the roof, some of the rides were able to be broken down into units and went up in the freight elevator, but not the slide, which was hoisted up outside the building. The slide—156 feet long, 36 feet high and 20 feet wide—had curves formed by laminated wood archways. All the rides had to be brought up and put into action overnight. On the opening Saturday, one thousand kids went down the slide in the first two and a half hours.

MARKET STREET FUN

After your visit with Santa, it was off to get a treat across the street at Woolworth's, which opened to great fanfare in 1952. When you entered the store, the smell of popcorn enticed you as you headed to check out the candy and nuts or to listen to 45rpm records before buying. Who could resist the downstairs food counter with its gooey pizza (with green onions), creamy old-fashioned milkshakes, hamburgers, cherry pies, hot dogs, popcorn, egg salad, hot turkey or tuna sandwiches? Or go for broke with a banana split. Then goof with your friends in the photo booth and check out the pet department downstairs with its hamsters, parakeets and goldfish.

After your lunch, it was time to walk up to Union Square to look at all the other windows, gaze in awe at the City of Paris's three-story Christmas tree and make a stop at Podesta Baldocchi to see all the ornaments and enjoy the smell of the pine wreaths.

A view from the Emporium on Market Street looking up Powell Street at the cable car turntable and Woolworth's. *SFMTA Photo | SFMTA.com/photo.*

Let's go back to the late 1800s, when the Emporium got its start. Its beginning didn't bode well, but it overcame its initial setbacks to become a retail powerhouse for many years.

A ROCKY START

For decades, the Emporium not only succeeded but thrived, despite near total destruction in the 1906 earthquake. After some business mishaps in the beginning, once the store was reorganized and managed as a single enterprise instead of a collection of individually owned small shops, it built a loyal clientele and was the place to go to shop, hear concerts, have a cup of tea or visit Santa.

In 1893, a German immigrant, Adolph Feist, leased the Parrott Building at 835 Market Street, with the idea of turning it into a large department store, hoping to interest an East Coast partner. Designed by San Francisco architect Albert Pissis, one of the first Americans to be trained at the École des Beaux Arts in Paris, the seven-story Parrott Building emulated the immense arcades of London and Paris. Pissis introduced the Beaux-Arts architectural style to San Francisco, designing a number of important buildings in the city in the years before and after the 1906 earthquake. In addition to the Emporium, Pissis designed the Hibernia Bank Building, the James Flood Building, the White House department store and the Mechanics' Institute.

In 1896, with great pomp, the Emporium opened. Some of the first businesses there were Nathan-Dohrmann & Co. (china, glassware, lamps and art goods), Kelly & Leibes (women's clothing) and Sing Fat & Co. (Chinese and Japanese bazaar). Offices, including the Supreme Court of California, occupied the upper floors.

Meanwhile, down the street, the Davis Brothers operated the Golden Rule Bazaar, a store selling "all lines of fancy goods, toys, notions, art goods, books, stationery, kid gloves, silver-plated ware, house-furnishing goods, gents' furnishing goods and hats."[95] Since its founding in 1871, the Golden Rule Bazaar had grown to be the largest establishment of its kind on the Pacific coast and one of the first in the United States.

Unfortunately, the original Emporium soon went bankrupt. It lacked centralized policy and management. F.W. Dohrmann, another German immigrant and a partner at Nathan-Dohrmann & Co. (and the author's

Above: The Emporium in its pre-earthquake grandeur. The store helped turn Market Street, with its excellent transportation, into a shopping destination. *Author's collection.*

Opposite, top: The Emporium's center court, with its glorious dome perched atop the building, and the stand in the middle with its café and bandstand. *Pam Gibson.*

Opposite, bottom: A woman peruses the many offerings on the selling floor in the jewelry department, circa 1898. Salesmen stand waiting for her order. *Louis Capecci.*

great-great-grandfather), saw possibilities in the store, in spite of the general opinion that any department store on the south side of the slot on Market Street must fail.

Dohrmann, along with some partners, also became interested in the Golden Rule Bazaar and merged the businesses, securing the bankrupt Emporium and moving the Golden Rule Bazaar to the Parrott Building. The new corporation included Dohrmann family members, plus Colonel M. Hecht, Albert Dernham, Henry Dernham, Marcus Gerstle, A.J. Hink, Andrew M. Davis and William Kaufman. The Emporium and Golden Rule Bazaar launched in September 1897. Andrew Davis and Henry Dernham were the managers. F.W. Dohrmann and his son, A.B.C. Dohrmann, helped build the management systems and procedures for different departments to work together.

As Dr. Carole Cosgrove Terry (another Dohrmann descendent) explains, in her short biography of Dohrmann:

Frederick W. "F.W." Dohrmann (1842–1914), a German immigrant, was instrumental in helping reorganize the Emporium into a prosperous department store with centralized management. *Author's collection.*

Dohrmann believed that the convenience of one building with separate departments, luxurious amenities such as attractive restrooms, resting and sitting rooms, art rooms and beautiful—often fantastic—décor would appeal to middle-class shoppers, not just the very wealthy. Marketing would target the middle class with such attractions as a tearoom where customers could dine while listening to an orchestra. He was attracted to the system of marked and fixed prices and money-back guarantees that signified a degree of trust between merchants and customers.[96]

In Dohrmann's own words, "To make such an enterprise profitable… it is necessary that we should have INTELLIGENT LEADERSHIP, PERFECT ORGANIZATION and AMPLE CAPITAL.…We must: ORGANIZE, CAPITALIZE, HARMONIZE, SYSTEMATIZE, ECONOMIZE and ADVERTISE."[97]

Soon, a well-knit organization was thriving, and the store became a popular social as well as shopping center, with band concerts every Saturday night. From 1898 to 1906, the Emporium's unbroken line of success put the enterprise up among the leaders of the city's retail trade.

Left: The Emporium's 1905–6 138-page mail-order catalogue, *The Emporium Economist*, included everything from furniture to clothing to flags. *Ron Ross.*

Below: The Emporium's café provided customers with a place to rest and socialize as waitresses in starched uniforms stood ready to bring tea or other food items. *Author's collection.*

In 1901, the Golden Rule Bazaar name was removed, and the operation simply became the Emporium.

The Emporium was an incredibly elegant store, with marble, bronze, steel and polished mahogany throughout. The ground floor was over 96,000 square feet and the rotunda 140 feet in diameter; 125 tons of steel went into the dome. Fifteen elevators serviced the upper floors, and over fifty miles of electric wire were installed. A newspaper article in 1896 declared:

> *San Francisco's Palatial Structure Excels the Famous Bon Marchés of Paris....The first view of the Emporium and the interior...is dreamlike. There is a vast blaze of electricity...10,000 lights—a vast expanse of white enameled wood that looks like marble, a street paved with a marble mosaic, as Pompeii was....Everything is a creamy white, but the 4,000 electric lights fringe the dome with sparkling color.*[98]

Concerts "under the Dome" were a big draw. A typical concert might be a three-hour Grand Matinee Concert offering twenty-one musical compositions. The store also provided a trained nurse who oversaw an emergency hospital and children's nursery. Mothers could leave their little boys in the barbershop to have their hair cut while they were shopping in other parts of the building.

WHO WAS F.W. DOHRMANN?

F.W. Dohrmann was a merchant who was respected among colleagues, employees and friends. Again, Dr. Carole Cosgrove Terry:

> *F.W. Dohrmann had arrived in San Francisco in 1862, when merchants and investors were busy building a regional empire in Northern California. Those with German roots were often among the merchants who dominated the wholesale and retail clothing, dry goods and crockery enterprises in the city. Dohrmann always proclaimed that he arrived with practically no money, calling himself a "poor German boy" who was teased about his strange clothes. Despite a lack of formal schooling, he had command of the English language. Because he could readily communicate with native-born English speakers, he was able to build a merchandising/import business for his German- and non-German-speaking neighbors, as well as serve as a volunteer for many of the city's philanthropic organizations.*[99]

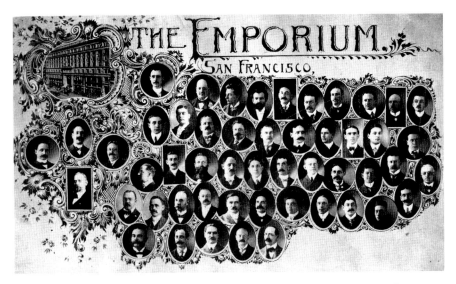

These portraits, although not identified, are probably of Emporium managers or buyers. F.W. Dohrmann believed that "justice tempered with kindness" was the way to treat employees. *Ron Ross.*

Dohrmann was involved in many commercial and civic ventures, including helping to organize the San Francisco Hotel Company, which operated the St. Francis Hotel, and leading the Merchants' Association. He served as a director for several of the Dohrmann Commercial Company's syndicate stores, as a member of the Park Commission and as a University of California regent.

In a 1913 memo, F.W. Dohrmann stated that "justice tempered with kindness" was the way to treat employees. The employees should know that "they are going to have a fair deal and candid recognition of good service, and the best compensation and advancement that there is to give them."[100]

An example of the management's generosity and attitude toward employees: they held annual balls under the dome for all employees, with management in attendance. As the *San Francisco Call* reported in 1899, "The music for the first dance was sounded at 9 o'clock, and from that time on till after midnight, when the last of eighteen numbers had been stepped off, the merriest time imaginable was had, with pleasant intermissions for little bites and many opportunities for little têtes-à-têtes."[101]

THE EARTHQUAKE AND ITS AFTERMATH

When the powerful quake hit in the early morning of April 18, 1906, the subsequent out-of-control fires caused the most damage. The Emporium, and most of Market Street, was devastated. Only the Emporium's front and dome survived. Newspapers all over the country were carrying the story of the great earthquake and fire that threatened to destroy the entire city of San Francisco. Reporters hurried from one scene to another. The fire burned continuously during Wednesday and Thursday (when its main progress was checked) and to a small extent on Friday and Saturday, April 18–21, 1906. In the histrionic tone typical of the era, one newspaper said that total annihilation seems to be San Francisco's fate, and "indescribable confusion" and "indescribable madness" reigned. "Thrilling rescues" and "deeds of valor would fill a volume."[102]

In a 1906 letter from Fred Dohrmann Jr. to his father, F.W., who was in New York at the time, he described the aftermath of the San Francisco earthquake and fire:

> *The Emporium…was burned out completely on Thursday morning. No salvage to merchandise or anything; all damage to their stock having been lost by fire….The loss of life in all this calamity was very small as was shown by recent figures, namely up to Saturday afternoon being only 333 and the inconvenience of living, great as they may seem, dwindle away in insignificance behind the new spirit which, like a Phoenix rising from the flames, seems to have entered into the mind and soul of each one for a greater and better San Francisco than ever before.*[103]

All of the Emporium's records were destroyed or lost with the exception of the accounts payable, which showed how much the store owed but not how much was owed to it. In order to collect its outstanding bills, the store advertised in the newspapers inviting customers to pay what they owed. It was a tribute to the loyalty of its customers that many customers voluntarily paid their bills, even though there was no written record of transactions. The U.S. Post Office mailed the records that were salvaged to the store because several quick-thinking employees had stuffed the records in a U.S. mailbag before fleeing the fire. The mailbags were dumped on Jessie Street and forgotten. A mail carrier passing by saw them and, thinking them to be mail, rescued them.

After the earthquake rocked the city, the ensuing inferno swept up 5th Street, destroying buildings like the Emporium and sending bursts of flame hundreds of feet into the air. *California History Room, California State Library, Sacramento, California.*

Emporium president F.W. Dohrmann returned immediately from his trip and became active in the rehabilitation of the city. He served on the finance committee that handled the Red Cross funds. Mayor Eugene Schmitz appointed F.W.'s son A.B.C. to be on the Committee of Fifty, which was composed of civic leaders, entrepreneurs, newspapermen and politicians to manage the crisis.

At first, European insurance companies refused to pay claims for fire damage for many San Francisco policyholders, believing that it was the quake that caused the damage (they didn't insure for earthquakes). In November 1906, F.W. Dohrmann, together with Oscar Sutro and William Thomas, went to Europe to negotiate with the insurance companies. They were instrumental in considerably increasing the insurance companies' payouts. As evidence, Dohrmann and the others took with them hundreds of photographs showing San Francisco before and after the earthquake and then after the fire.

SETTING UP SHOP ON VAN NESS AVENUE

Store management immediately set about finding temporary quarters for the store, which managed to reopen in May 1906 in a residence owned by one of the Emporium's stockholders, Elias Hecht, at Van Ness Avenue and Post Street. One of the bathrooms served as the business office, and the employment office was in the clothes closet. The entire house was used, including the stable and hot house, as well as an annex they built in the rear. The two-story building ended up having almost as much selling space as on Market Street, making the salesroom again the largest on the coast, if not the largest west of Chicago.

F. S. "Daddy" Owles, who was then at the New York office, sent carloads of merchandise immediately, so the Emporium was the first department store to reopen after the fire. This speedy delivery of merchandise was a real inspiration to the revival of trade in San Francisco.

The Emporium set up its temporary headquarters on Van Ness Avenue, a north–south thoroughfare running from Market Street north to the Bay. *Pam Gibson.*

The entire house was used as a temporary headquarters. One of the bathrooms served as the business office, and the employment office was in the clothes closet. *California History Room, California State Library, Sacramento, California.*

The store not only survived but prospered. Henry Dernham, general manager, said that the sales volume was far greater than he had expected or dared to hope for, and "it seemed as though the only limit was in the ability of Emporium buyers to secure merchandise and in acquiring sufficient space in which to handle both goods and customers."[104]

A GRAND REOPENING

The city was quickly rebuilt and soon had a cleaner and more modern look. The fire had destroyed the slums south of Market, and the old Victorian downtown was gone. Within weeks, streetcars were running on Market Street. By July, the Chronicle newspaper company was back in its former headquarters. By August, the California Street Cable Railroad Co. had repaired its powerhouse, put the cable machinery back in order and was running cable cars to the top of Nob Hill again.

The Emporium operated in its temporary buildings until the fall of 1908, when a rebuilt Emporium on Market Street reopened to great fanfare on October 1. The store invited the public to come through the portals of the past (the original doors) into the store of the present. It was

MARKET STREET, THE GREAT HIGHWAY OF THE CITY'S TRAFFIC, WHERE TROLLEY HAS SUCCEEDED CABLE AND WHERE STONE AND STEEL HAVE RISEN ON THE ASHES OF WOODEN BUILDINGS. THE EMPORIUM, REBUILT WITH ITS OLD FACADE BY THE JAMES STEWART COMPANY, OPENED A MONTH AHEAD OF ITS EXPECTATION

The company made a special effort to include all the latest ideas in department store construction and arrangement in its new store, which opened in 1908. *SFMTA Photo | SFMTA.com/photo.*

built along the same lines as the original but on a much grander scale. At first, two floors were sufficient selling space, with the others leased to offices. As business boomed, however, the store expanded rapidly. The Basement Salesroom, which opened in 1911, covered forty thousand square feet and sold lower-priced goods drawn from every department in the house, with the exception of men's clothing. The store soon expanded to other floors and had an auditorium on the third floor with a seating capacity of five hundred people. As a 1916 newspaper article said, "The question is not 'What can I buy?' but 'What can't I buy?'"[105]

An article about the store's reopening in 1908 describes the ground floor:

The dry goods department is located at the front entrance, occupying the space at both sides of the central aisles, and reaches back two-thirds of the main floor. The shoe department, with its tall glass cases, which give it seclusion from prying eyes, is across the aisle from the dry goods department. Across the aisle from that department is one filled with the best and choicest garments for boys and children and reaches to the department for men's clothing. There are three broad entrances facing Market

Under the Emporium dome was an ideal place to meet friends, hear a concert or have tea in downtown San Francisco. *Louis Capecci.*

Street and five aisles running parallel with the center aisle. The most complete grocery and delicatessen departments known are also located on the first floor.[106]

With over sixty different departments, the Emporium promoted itself as the "Rainy Day Shopping Place," stating in ads, "We sell everything that man, woman or child can eat, wear or use in their houses."

By 1918, despite the demands of wartime, the Emporium had opened a nine-story annex building. The new "service annex" included employees' quarters, recreation rooms, a roof garden, children's playgrounds, a library, medical and dental quarters, cafés, a billiard room and offices. Many Emporium employees served in the war, and the store held events for Red Cross, Liberty Loans and the Food Conservation program (which included Victory Gardens, "wheatless Wednesdays" and "meatless Mondays").

THE 1920s AND 1930s: MERGING WITH CAPWELL AND SURVIVING THE ECONOMIC DOWNTURN

During the postwar '20s, the Emporium's fast growth continued. Americans' standard of living kept rising, and what better way to spend money than on household goods, clothing and luxury items such as wristwatches, electronics (phonographs and radios), perfumes and cosmetics? Nearly two thousand employees worked the Emporium's 600,000-square-foot store. Sales reached $16.8 million in 1925. It was an exciting time for America and for retail.

In 1927, plans were in the works for a Bay Bridge linking San Francisco to the East Bay (completed in 1936), and expanding the store to the East Bay made sense. That year, to great fanfare, the Emporium merged with the H.C. Capwell Company of Oakland, forming a holding company, the Emporium-Capwell Company. The two divisions merged their New York and overseas buying offices but operated their stores independently for many years.

H.C. Capwell was an Oakland institution. In 1899, Harris Cebert "H.C." Capwell opened a small store there called the Lace House. It changed its name to the H.C. Capwell Company two years later, moved to larger quarters and, as time progressed, was recognized as one of the leading retail stores in the Bay Area. By 1929, the merged organization had built a six-story building that became Capwell's largest store, located on a block of land in downtown Oakland.

By the late '20s, chain stores such as JCPenney and Sears were on the rise. JCPenney had 4 stores in 1908 and 1,452 by 1930. Sears, Roebuck & Company, which started as a mail-order house, opened its first 8 retail stores in 1925 and operated 338 by 1930. Sears established its stores away from large cities, with expansive parking lots. Downtown department stores such as the Emporium faced daunting challenges as their costs increased, traffic snarled the roadways and customers chose to move to the suburbs. Then the 1929 stock market crash and ensuing Great Depression hit, and consumers' disposable income all but evaporated. However, the Emporium weathered the downturn, enticing customers with visits from celebrities, radio programs, Christmas festivities, a traveling exhibition of "Treasures of the Czars" and a 1931 exhibit featuring a fifty-four-foot replica of the Golden Gate Bridge.

These elegant 1920s ladies in their fur coats stand in the entryway to the Emporium. *Jim Dickson.*

THE 1940s AND 1950s: WARTIME EFFORTS AND SUBURBAN EXPANSION

After the attack on Pearl Harbor in December 1941, Emporium employees were busy blacking out the dome, windows and light wells; organizing for civic defense; enrolling in first aid classes; and saying goodbye to more and more employees as they entered the service. From 1942 to 1945, the American Women's Voluntary Service (AWVS) Bond Booth sold bonds on the first floor. In the fall of 1945, with the war over, the Emporium was able to complete some deferred maintenance: for the first time since before the war, it was possible to clean, repair and paint the front of the store—a sign of peaceful days again.

In the years following World War II, the move to the suburbs and population growth created the need for more convenient retail shopping. Families moving to new housing developments away from city centers wanted shopping options. By 1950, virtually all major department store

Shoppers could get their very own Civil Defense Survival Kits at the Emporium during the height of the Cold War in the early 1960s. *SFMTA Photo* | *SFMTA.com/photo.*

Left: In the 1950s, women did not wear skirts or dresses without the proper bras, panties and slips, which the Emporium was happy to supply. *Ron Ross.*

Below: The friendly telephone operators at the Emporium could connect you to departments within the store. *Jim Dickson.*

In 1950, construction was underway for the new Emporium department store branch at Stonestown in the Lake Merced area. *San Francisco History Center, San Francisco Public Library.*

companies had committed to branch development, and the Emporium was no different. The company began its aggressive branch store expansion throughout the Bay Area.

On April 12, 1950, workers broke ground in the Stonestown Shopping Center in western San Francisco for the first branch store, six miles from its downtown parent. The three-level store, with extensive parking areas, opened in 1952. The company continued its rapid expansion into the suburbs with Capwell's Walnut Creek (1954), the Stanford Center Store (1956) in Palo Alto, Capwell's Hayward (1957) and Emporium Stevens Creek (1957). Each of the stores had over 200,000 square feet of space for goods and services and lots of room for parking.

THE 1960s AND BEYOND: SO WHAT HAPPENED?

Emporium kept opening branch stores into the late '60s: Hillsdale, Santa Rosa, Fremont, Almaden and other suburban locations. The inner city continued to decline in the '50s and '60s, while the suburbs boomed. From 1961 to the end of 1970, over 240 regional malls were built, more than three times the number that had been constructed in the previous fifteen years. Meanwhile, nationwide, traffic problems contributed to a decline in downtown retail business. Department stores located in downtown areas, fighting the decline of the inner cities, often had to cut back on some of their amenities such as tearooms, doormen and children's playrooms.

By 1969, when Broadway-Hale Stores (later Carter Hawley Hale Stores, or CHH), based in Southern California, acquired Emporium-Capwell Co., there were eleven branch stores, plus the downtown Emporium in San Francisco and H.C. Capwell Co. in Oakland. The Emporium-Capwell acquisition was part of CHH's buying binge that included Neiman Marcus and the Walden Book Co. CHH tripled sales between 1968 and 1973, and in 1984, CHH was the sixth-largest department store chain firm in the United States.

Disaster struck in 1989 when the San Francisco earthquake damaged most of the Emporium stores. All closed temporarily, and Emporium's downtown Oakland store remained closed for most of its fiscal year. By 1991, burdened by significant debt from its too-rapid expansion and unable to refurbish the drab, outdated stores to keep up with the competition and retailing trends, CHH sought bankruptcy protection.

Despite a reorganization under financier Sam Zell, renaming the corporation Broadway Stores, the company still struggled. In August 1995, Federated Department Stores, which owned Macy's, acquired Broadway Stores. Federated dissolved the chain in 1996 and consolidated the former Emporium, Broadway and Weinstock's stores, along with its own Macy's California and Bullock's chains, to form Macy's West. The grand dame of Market Street was no more.

A GRAND REVITALIZATION

The beautiful building sat sadly empty for many years, until developers Forest City Enterprises and the Westfield Group razed it in 2003 in preparation for a new mall, the Westfield San Francisco Centre. They preserved the Neoclassical façade and the dome. To keep the dome safe while the building was under construction, a custom hydraulic system lifted the 500,000-pound dome to perch on a supporting tower, where it waited for almost a year while the new structure was built underneath it. Its final resting place was 58 feet from its original position, which allowed natural light through its crown and lunette windows. There are over eight hundred glass panels in the dome and more than nine hundred lights encased in its structural ribs. The three-story dome is the centerpiece of a 200-foot-long, 65-foot-wide atrium and colonnade. It is 98 feet from the floor of the grand rotunda, which begins on the fourth floor of the Centre, to the top of the dome's ceiling. The dome sits about 168 feet above Market and Mission Streets.

In addition to the façade and dome, the developers restored many of the period features. The cast-iron window system, sandstone walls, columns, historic wood windows and glazing were completely restored. The revived street-level features display windows, bronze doors and copper piping, all elements that were part of the 1908 look of the store. Balustrades that had been removed are again prominent at the building's cornice and over the main entry of the fourth floor.

After years of negotiations, bureaucratic wrangling and reconstruction, the new mall, a $440 million retail-office-entertainment complex, opened in September 2006. The Centre, anchored by Nordstrom and Bloomingdale's, is 1.5 million square feet, triple the Emporium's original size because Westfield took over adjoining space.

THE EMPORIUM LEGACY

A few years ago, while working on my earlier Emporium book (Arcadia Publishing, 2014), I was surprised at the depth of nostalgia for the old store. I met many people who had their first jobs or spent their entire careers there or were regular shoppers, often with their mothers and grandmothers. At one book signing, a group of former employees showed up, a few wearing their Emporium badges!

Many salespeople worked there for their entire careers, including Sara Lee Cohen, who worked at the store for decades, starting in 1939. Richard Parker, who worked mostly in shoes until 1993, says that Cohen used to entertain him with detailed stories about the store:

> We would sometimes take a break together and go downstairs to pick up some food. We would walk through the store, past the dome, past millinery and take the escalators down. She would tell stories about what the store was like in the '40s and '50s in great detail. "See these columns, these used to have bouquets of fresh flowers." She went on and on. She was a character.

Parker says that when Marian and Vivian Brown, the identical twins known for walking around San Francisco in their striking matching outfits, made their visits to the Emporium (about twice a month), they would always check in with Sara Lee. They all wore the same style wig, a platinum flip-style hairdo like actress Dina Merrill's. Another longtime employee was Jayne Gygi, the Emporium's "Lady at the Info Booth" just inside the main entrance. These ladies were all "the voice of experience" when helping customers.

Drew Howard, whose father, Andrew Howard, worked at the Market Street Emporium starting in 1953 and later at Stonestown, gave me a scrapbook that his father kept with all his Emporium mementos. Employee newsletters (*The Big E Life*), congratulatory notes from co-workers, his staff IDs, goodbye cards, poems—Andrew saved them all. He was very proud of working there and kept all the notes he received when he was promoted. He was also quite the innovator and submitted many entries to the "Effective Ideas" suggestion box. How about a barbershop so men have something to do while their wives shop? Ads throughout a department promoting complementary items located in other departments? How about a Christmas club? Women's hosiery packaged in portable capsule containers? (This was before the days of L'Eggs hosiery.) Credit applications at all service desks? Although he had many ideas, the only one it looks like he won a prize for (fifteen dollars) was the suggestion that salespeople, on closing a sale, should say, "Shall I leave the shoes in the box or just put them in one of our convenient carrying bags?" This precluded the customer asking to have her package sent.

I also connected with Gloria Frere, who started in the Santa Rosa store in 1966 doing alterations, and she says it was the best place to have a job, grow up and have a family. She was promoted to alterations manager, then went to the bridal department and finally to a role as executive secretary. She says it was a bygone era; things were much simpler. Employees really had fun together, having parties and participating in community activities like building floats for a parade. Gloria stressed that the store had a strong people-oriented culture—it was "all about the people." The Santa Rosa store was a model store that performed well, but that couldn't help save the chain. However, even after the company folded, the former employees got together for reunions, which would have gladdened the heart of co-founder F.W. Dohrmann, who said:

Success means to gain distinction in one's own calling; to gain the respect and good will of those with whom we come in contact; to do justice to our fellow workers; to deal fairly with those who compete with us or occupy similar or rival positions, who must not be treated as enemies but rather as friends from whom we must learn how to be successful or how to avoid failure, but whose respect we must always deserve and if possible retain; and finally to obtain the best possible financial compensation for one's efforts. [107]

Chapter 6

JOSEPH MAGNIN, 1913–1984

"Quality is Remembered
Long After Price is Forgotten"

I t's the holiday season, 1969. You're a busy executive who works in the Financial District, and as usual, you are at a total loss about a gift for your wife or perhaps the other women in your life. Going into stores on your own is a bit overwhelming, and half the time you know the gift gets returned anyway.

Imagine your delight when you hear about Joseph Magnin's (JM) new department, the Wolves' Den. An area of the store just for men, where attractive young women serve you cocktails and others search the store to bring possible gifts to you to peruse and purchase. Promoted as a shopping refuge, accessible only by invitation, the Wolves' Den was "a special gentlemen's shopping retreat filled with gifts from throughout JM, helpful hostesses & spirited refreshments."[108]

Fifty years later, it's doubtful such an enterprise would fit today's cultural mores. Even in 1969, the Wolves' Den was in keeping with JM's sassy marketing and distinct brand (although the department was as much about reducing returns as increasing sales).

JM was known as the fun place to shop, and the Wolves' Den was one of its typical innovations. The store wanted its clientele to see the stores as "alive, fresh, elegant, modern, exciting, fun-to-shop at, cosmopolitan," providing a "top-to-toe-look and flair," as a JM marketing study[109] stated.

Who was Joseph Magnin, and how did this store make such an impact in San Francisco and the West? And why, if it had over thirty stores in 1969, did the Joseph Magnin name disappear by 1984?

A MERCHANDISING DYNASTY

Ellen Magnin Newman has a pillow in her office that says, "Less Is a Bore." On the wall hangs a sign: "Quality is Remembered Long After Price is Forgotten." The granddaughter of Joseph Magnin and daughter of Cyril Magnin, Ellen was intricately involved with the store from childhood.

Joseph, born in 1866, was the third child (second son) of Isaac and Mary Ann Magnin's eight children. Mary Ann founded I. Magnin in 1876, and the Magnin brood worked sweeping floors, marking merchandise and making deliveries. Over the years, there was stiff competition among the Magnin boys for their mother's favor and for desirable roles in the store. Mary Ann ruled the store and didn't tolerate any shenanigans.

Joseph liked the ladies and, as his son, Cyril, related in his autobiography,[110] got in some trouble in his early years. One story goes that Joseph, who was about sixteen years old at the time, was sent out to deliver some very expensive lingerie COD. When he arrived at the delivery address, a woman in a very transparent negligee opened the door. He ended up in bed with two women. When it was time for him to go, he asked for the lingerie money, and he was told he had gotten his money's worth and to get out. Joseph knew his mother would be furious, so he borrowed the money to cover the costs of the package. It took him two years to pay it off.

In 1892, Mary Ann chose her younger son John, who was twenty-two, to manage the Market Street I. Magnin store, bypassing his older brothers Samuel and Joseph. Cyril recalled that John was as "stubborn, bossy and single-minded as his mother, and he and my father would have jurisdictional

Joseph Magnin, Mary Ann and Isaac Magnin's second son, struck out on his own in 1913 to create a store to compete with I. Magnin. *San Francisco History Center, San Francisco Public Library.*

Joseph first bought into Newman & Levinson, located at Stockton and O'Farrell Streets. He soon changed the name to Newman-Magnin. *San Francisco History Center, San Francisco Public Library.*

battles all the time."[111] In 1898, Joseph transgressed once again, this time by falling in love and marrying Charlotte (Lottie) Davis, the head milliner at I. Magnin. Fraternizing with the help was a big no-no to start with, and marriage went far beyond fraternizing. Mary Ann was not pleased.

By 1913, Joseph had had enough and decided it was time to strike out on his own. He bought into a store called Newman & Levinson, which sold piece goods, buttons and notions, located at Stockton and O'Farrell Streets. He changed the name to Newman-Magnin and by 1918 had bought out his partners. The name became Joseph Magnin Co. Mary Ann, not known for her generous spirit, was furious that Joseph had set up a competing store, and there was very little contact between the families for many years. Joseph Magnin positioned itself as a midrange seller of apparel and millinery, but it was difficult to compete with I. Magnin, the grand dame a few blocks away, especially since I. Magnin forbid other suppliers from working with JM, which hampered their buying efforts, to say the least.

CYRIL

Despite the hard work of Joseph, Lottie and their son Cyril, the store's fortunes in the '20s and '30s were precarious. It was Lottie's millinery business that helped them survive. Cyril, born in 1899, was involved in every aspect of the store, and by the mid-'30s, he had some ideas about how to reposition the store so it could thrive. At first Joseph resisted, but by 1938, he relented and gave Cyril permission to try something new.

What was Cyril's big idea? It was time to go after a new market: youth. No more matronly styles. The city was changing. Cyril noticed, as the city mobilized for war, that the influx of lots of servicemen, their families and girlfriends was changing the demographics. And after the war, there was going to be pent-up demand and they would have money to spend.

Cyril loved the Wolves' Den, a shopping refuge for men only, where lovely ladies served cocktails while men smoked cigars and considered their shopping options. *San Francisco History Center, San Francisco Public Library.*

Cyril Magnin, "Mr. San Francisco," was the creative merchandising force behind Joseph Magnin's re-branding as the *fun* place to shop. *San Francisco History Center, San Francisco Public Library.*

Cyril, who was almost forty years old at this point and feeling JM was in a rut with its merchandising, reconfigured the store. Out went the larger sizes and dowdy fashions. However, even though they were going after a younger market, quality was still of paramount importance (remember Ellen Magnin Newman's "Quality is Remembered Long After Price is Forgotten" pillow?).

And it worked. They carved a distinct niche for themselves—JM was *the* fun place to shop—and soon people were taking notice. In 1954, for example, instead of shopping at the higher-end I. Magnin, Marilyn Monroe purchased a suit (black with a white ermine collar) at JM to wear for her wedding to Joe DiMaggio. Cyril and his family were the driving force.

MR. SAN FRANCISCO

Cyril Magnin, who first studied to be an attorney, found his calling as a master merchandiser who drove JM to be innovative and ahead of the game. He and his wife, Anna (and soon his three children, Donald, Ellen and Jerry), were the hardworking, creative forces behind the JM style. As Ellen says of her father, "He liked young people as friends and family and employees. He really had a sense of adventure." Cyril had an open-door policy and encouraged an atmosphere of "creative anarchy." He gave the people working for him a lot of leeway to try new things, even if some of them failed.

> *He was a very savvy merchandiser, and loved to hire young people, especially women, and set them loose to be creative and learn responsibility. They didn't have to punch a clock, but they were expected to produce. As Isla Adams, a former personnel director said, "To a person, we all felt we owned the store. That sink or swim, we were going to contribute. We took it very personally."*[112]

Cyril wanted to be first with the best. He walked to work every day and was well known around San Francisco for his many decades of civic volunteer work and philanthropy. (When Cyril died in 1988 at the age of eighty-eight, a street was named after him, Cyril Magnin Street.) He became the city's first chief of protocol, serving twenty-two years, a volunteer position where he greeted visiting dignitaries and made arrangements for them to have the best San Francisco experience possible. He was a regular at the opera and *Beach Blanket Babylon*, the long-running San Francisco stage show, which had a Cyril Magnin seating section, as he reportedly attended 464 performances.

He loved his dog, Robbie, a Cairn terrier, and young Nancy Bacall remembers that when she was hired at the age of seventeen, one of her duties was to walk Cyril's dog. She also wrapped presents for Cyril, including a pair of shoes for either Ladybird or one of the Johnson daughters. (Cyril was a friend of President Lyndon Johnson, and Johnson's daughter Lynda got her trousseau from JM in 1967.)

> *I think they were a size 14. That was the most unusual package that I wrapped for him* [because the shoes were so big].... *Whatever they needed in the executive offices I did. It was such a fun, lively job that I took it more seriously than I did my school work. I also remember buying a paper dress from JM. There was a time in the '70s that they were making clothing out of paper and I bought it and wore it to a party.*

Nancy also wrapped presents in the Wolves' Den, the men-only boutique: "The guys would tip very nicely. Sometimes I would walk home with a ten-dollar tip."

Ellen says of her father, "He hired the first Japanese employee in San Francisco after World War II when they were let out of the camps. He proved to be an invaluable employee....Cyril always made the more adventurous decision." And she adds, "Almost everyone in the receiving room was a refugee from Germany. They were a whole crew; their own mafia. Just recently a couple of them stopped me on the street. I couldn't believe it."

Cyril was also the markdown king. He believed if a product didn't move in two weeks, it wouldn't improve with age: "We're not selling antiques; we're not selling wine. Get rid of it."[113]

THE MAGNIN TEAM

Joseph Magnin Co. was a group effort. At first, Anna Smithline Magnin, Cyril's wife, a very fashionable woman with a distinct sense of style, worked tirelessly alongside him. Her early death was devastating, but Cyril's children, Ellen, Donald and Jerry, stepped up.

As Ellen says, "The great misfortune in my life and the life of Joseph Magnin was that my mother died very suddenly at the age of forty-eight when I was twenty, and my father was going to sell the company. He said, 'I can't go on without your mother.' I said, 'Yes, you can. *I* can do it.'"

Ellen first "worked" at the store when she was three years old, in 1931. As she says about her grandfather, the founder:

> *Joseph was very penurious. He had the first penny he ever earned. In those days, you could mail a letter within San Francisco for two cents, but out of town was three cents. They taught me to read C-I-T-Y* [i.e., San Francisco], *and I sorted all the customer bills that said C-I-T-Y into one pile and my brother Donald, a year and a half older, got all the others and he would sort San Mateo and Palo Alto. My grandfather would drop them in the local* [two-cent] *mail*[box] *as he rode home to Los Altos.*

Joseph Magnin's flagship store stood out on the corner of Stockton and O'Farrell in the mid-1970s. *San Francisco History Center, San Francisco Public Library.*

She continues, "Before I worked on the staff, I worked on the switchboard. I was a telephone operator. I worked in the credit department. And I left Stanford in my senior year—I never graduated—in order to help out after my mother died." Cyril agreed to let her take on a greater role, and she turned out to have a savvy, creative eye for what would appeal to their target market.

One of Ellen's favorite stories: On a New York trip to see the manufacturers that her mother had done business with, one manufacturer she visited was "making a peacoat and it was black and velveteen, and I said, 'I don't like black,' and he said, 'What do you want, Miss Magnin?' I said, 'I want orange, lemon and lime, like Jell-O.' And they made orange, lemon and lime velveteen, and Joseph Magnin literally sold thousands of them. We only had a few stores then, but they converted the rest of the country into color....It changed the market and changed the public's view on how they could look." No more dark green, navy or maroon.

The family held different titles over the years, but basically Ellen was the chain's director of creative merchandising; her older brother Donald was executive vice president in charge of merchandising; her husband, Walter Newman, was senior vice president for operations and development; and her younger brother Jerry was the southern division vice president.

Walter Newman, whom Ellen Magnin married in 1950, handled the intricacies of the company's real estate negotiations during their rapid expansion. "He was a financial real estate man," says Ellen. "When my father asked him to come into the business, he said we were a bunch of creative geniuses and we're also crazy—thinking he'd settle us down—and he did."

KINKY, KICKY, KOOKY

JM's advertising department broke all the rules. The ads were anything but staid. Instead, they were edgy, witty, colorful and full of movement. Who was the JM woman? Full hair, big eyes, forward-thinking. During the '60s, Betty Brader Ashley became one of the chief illustrators, and her distinct style is what is remembered about the JM "look." Art director Marget Larson and Brader Ashley were "an incomparable team," says Ellen. Ashley won many awards for her innovative illustrations, and a selection of her Joseph Magnin advertisements, posters and store decorations is in the Smithsonian's National Museum of American History.

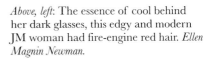

Above, left: The essence of cool behind her dark glasses, this edgy and modern JM woman had fire-engine red hair. *Ellen Magnin Newman.*

Above, right: Fresh, innovative designs aimed at the upwardly mobile younger woman were a core component of Joseph Magnin's branding. *Ellen Magnin Newman.*

Middle: The boxes were more efficient than wrapping, as they took less time; customers could assemble their boxes at home. *Ellen Magnin Newman.*

Bottom: Joseph Magnin's customers looked forward each holiday season to the latest designs in JM's award-winning Christmas boxes, which became collectors' items. *Ellen Magnin Newman.*

JM, always looking to try something new, used bright colors (like Ellen's peacoats), in its ads, which was unusual. The art director and artists would go down to the newspaper and make sure they were doing it properly. They also took unusual placements, like the "gutter" in a newspaper spread (in the center). Some ads would take up almost the entire two-page spread, and if the ad didn't take the entire space, there usually wasn't enough space for another ad in what was left.

Their award-winning Christmas boxes, initially designed by Marget Larson, were collectors' items. However, they weren't just for show; they were more practical than wrapping, as it took less time for the salespeople. Customers could assemble their boxes at home, although the salesperson would do it if asked. Over the years there were pyramids, a gingerbread toy land village, a design adapted from antiquarian book endpapers, a trunk, a photo album and a Tom and Jerry mug. "Christmasdipity," a two-piece apparel box looking like a picnic basket, won the Gold Award in 1966 from the Folding Paper Box Association of America.

Edgy visuals extended beyond the advertising to stores. For instance, in the mid-'60s, during the height of the Peter Max bright-color psychedelic craze, JM painted the store walls in pop art colors, salesgirls wore mini-skirts and store graphics were theatrically psychedelic.

LEADING THE WAY

"Joseph Magnin was always ahead of the pack," says Ellen. The company moved quickly and was at the forefront with many innovations, including paper dresses, a wear-it-once craze of the '60s, and Rudy Gernreich's 1964 topless swimsuit. Ellen noted that her brother Jerry Magnin introduced a small electronics boutique in the men's department, featuring Sony portable radios.

To keep merchandise moving, they opened Magnarama in 1962 on the sixth floor of the main store. Markdowns from all seventeen stores filled the 2,500-square-foot selling space, discounted for quick sale. No returns allowed. To repeat Cyril's maxim, "We're not selling antiques; we're not selling wine. Get rid of it." His usual philosophy was that the customer was king—always right—and returns were accepted; however, the point of Magnarama was to move the merchandise.

In 1971, to much fanfare, JM launched a Gucci department in the San Francisco store. When it opened, there was such a crowd that Cyril helped

JM's holiday boxes took many forms, from cakes, pyramids or a gingerbread toy land village to photo albums and picnic baskets. *Ellen Magnin Newman.*

out on the selling floor because they were shorthanded. At a VIP reception, Cyril opened a Gucci briefcase and presented Dr. Aldo Gucci with a key to the city. It was the first time Gucci had opened under the auspices of another store, and Joseph Magnin felt it added prestige to be able to offer the harness-trimmed shoes, scarves, jewelry, handbags and luggage to status seekers. Soon there were Gucci departments in many other Joseph Magnin stores, and JM controlled some freestanding Gucci stores as well.

GOING, GOING, GONE

Innovation and growth were the driving forces from the late '30s on. By 1928, JM had opened its first branch, in Palo Alto, California. It focused on the suburbs, where stores could have more impact. After the Reno store opened in 1940, other stores followed in quick succession: San Mateo, 1942; Sacramento, 1946; Oakland, 1948; Cal-Neva, Nevada, 1950; and on and on until there were approximately thirty-one stores by the late '60s. All were in California and Nevada, as that was the strategy. And Cyril firmly believed in a formula for low-cost leases, saying, "The curse of the retail business is putting money into fixed assets. Our policy is to put our money into merchandise and accounts receivable. We don't tie up funds in store-owned fixtures."[114]

When a store opened, they aimed for a lot of buzz. In 1970, at the opening of the Palm Springs store, Liberace attended the ribbon-cutting ceremony, along with Miss Palm Springs.

They made a move into Las Vegas in 1957. Says Ellen:

> In Las Vegas, every store had been within a casino. Cyril wanted a freestanding store. And he said, "Walter [Newman], I want you to go to Las Vegas, meet these people; I think they'll build us a store." I can never forget when Walter and I went to Las Vegas with the mob. Walter had to play golf with them. And I think the most Walter played golf for was $5 a hole. And when he got to Las Vegas they said, "We play for $5," and Walter said, "Well, I play for $5 all the time." The guy said, "This is $500, Walter." This was Mo Dalitz, who became our landlord eventually. Walter said, "Mo, I don't play for $500." Then Mo said, "Then what are you going to play for?" Walter said, "Well, I'm used to playing for $5." Dalitz said, "OK, I'll pick up the $495." The whole day he was playing for $995. So Walter played for $5 and Walter played the best golf he ever played in his life. And they all paid cash in the end to Mo Dalitz.
>
> They shook hands, and though Mo is often described as a Mafioso, his goal was to keep the Mafia out of Las Vegas, to keep crime out of Las Vegas. And there were all these dreadful things written about him, but Walter always said he was the most honest man he ever knew. They shook hands; they never had a written contract. They built the most unbelievable building next to the Desert Inn.

And so JM got its store in Las Vegas.

They broke ground for the Las Vegas store in January 1957 and opened at 1:15 a.m. on August 31, 1957. Why 1:15 a.m.?

The Las Vegas opening was one of Ellen's most memorable successes. She says that when Mo Dalitz, their landlord, heard they were planning on doing their grand opening during the day, he said, "I don't think you understand this city. We can have Bob Hope playing golf with Bing Crosby and nobody comes. It's daylight. Nobody is awake during the day." So Ellen looked at everybody and said, "Then let's open it around midnight." They actually closed up the highways between South LA and Las Vegas because the crowds were so big, with about eleven thousand people coming to the midnight opening. Milton Berle was the master of ceremonies, and actress Jane Powell cut the ribbon. Designers Oleg Cassini, Harvey Berin, Herbert Sondheim, Herbert and Beth Levine and Cyril's sister-in-law, Adele Simpson (Anna's sister), were flown in.

Not only was the opening a wild success, but according to Ellen, "We changed the dress habits of the women in Las Vegas. Prior to Joseph Magnin, everybody wore dyed-to-match sweaters, skirts and shoes—pastels, mainly."

SO WHAT HAPPENED?

The growth and marketing strategy worked. Joseph Magnin Co.'s sales boomed, jumping from $17 million in 1957 to $47 million in 1967. The company went public (the Magnin family retained majority control) in 1960. However, they faced some serious decisions about growth, as they felt they had saturated markets in California and Nevada. But did they really want to expand into other markets? Chicago? New York? That would have been a huge, risky move.

By 1969, they had over thirty stores, and although the family wasn't looking to sell, suitors were making offers. One that they couldn't ignore was from AMFAC (American Factors, Ltd.), based in Honolulu, which offered over $30 million, three and a half times earnings, a very high price. AMFAC, which was looking to expand to the mainland, had many companies in its portfolio covering a range of industries, from sugar cane production to construction machinery, hotels, restaurants and department stores, including Liberty House, a department store chain also based in Honolulu. AMFAC said it wanted JM's management team and reputation, and part of the deal was keeping the company's management team in place. They signed five-year contracts. It all sounded good, and everyone wanted to see the stores succeed in the national marketplace.

It was soon apparent that Magnin's "creative anarchy" management style was markedly different than AMFAC's buttoned-up corporate style. AMFAC also turned out to have a totally different merchandising approach. Within six months, the Magnin executive team was demoted and offered lesser positions. For example, Jerry, who had been vice president of the southern division, was told to return to San Francisco to be an assistant merchandise manager. This didn't sit well, and in 1970, the Magnins and Newmans left the company.

AMFAC's approach to marketing, according to a 1982 article, "How Corporate Gray Collided with the Flash and Dash at Joseph Magnin,"[115] was to discern customer needs and wants and respond by having the right merchandise. JM, on the other hand, held the opposite view: study your customer's lifestyle and then tell her what to wear. Their approach to real estate varied wildly too. As mentioned before, Cyril Magnin never bought property; JM leased its stores, low rents plus a profit percentage, from landlords who built and equipped them. AMFAC signed leases with high rents and built some of its own stores, investing $20 million.

AMFAC moved ahead with expansion plans, pushing into new markets from Hawaii to Utah and by 1977 had forty-eight stores and an after-tax loss of $16 million. This didn't bode well. AMFAC sold JM to Hillman Company in 1977 for $28 million, incurring more than $17 million in losses after taxes. Five years later, it was sold to Acquihold Corp., of La Jolla, another investment company.

During 1982 and 1983, more stores closed. The San Francisco store decreased its selling space from six floors to three. Finally, in September 1984, the company filed for bankruptcy, closing twenty-two stores and putting over 850 employees out of work. As Cyril Magnin said to one of the AMFAC executives, "Joseph Magnin is like a finely tuned clock. And if you start playing with it, it's going to stop ticking."[116] And that's just what happened.

THE BEAT GOES ON

The legacy of Joseph Magnin lives on. In 1999, about three hundred former employees, one of whom came from as far as Chile, got together for a reunion dinner in San Francisco. Some of them have gone on to found their own retail ventures, such as Sue Fisher King, who has a high-end home accessories shop on Sacramento Street, and Marsha Lasky and Sharon Leach, who own Sweet Things bakery on California Street. Emily Lee, a former sportswear buyer, also had a shop in San Francisco.

Sally Erlanger Gerstein, who went on to a career in retail as well, worked at Joseph Magnin when she was about twenty years old, in the early '70s. When asked about her most distinct memory, she says it was when she was assigned to the lingerie department, and one of her first customers was a transvestite in search of a girdle. Sally kept asking the customer, who was in the fitting room, how things were going, and got the response, "Sweetie, I'm just fine."

Cyril Magnin would be proud to know that all those young workers whom he encouraged to be innovative and then let loose have gone on to their own successes. After JM, Cyril's own family continued to have very successful marketing and retail careers.

EPILOGUE

The demise of these stores definitely followed certain patterns. It's tempting to play the "if only" game. If only the next generation of the families who founded the old stores had been interested in continuing the tradition… if only the families hadn't sold to a corporate entity that changed the character of the stores…if only they hadn't expanded so quickly, depleting cash and taking on too much risk…if only real estate in San Francisco hadn't gotten so pricey. And on and on. But the reality is that the grand downtown department stores no longer have a place in the retail panorama. Department stores across the United States have been losing market share for decades to changing shopping habits, e-commerce, discount chains and other retailing upstarts. It's a brutal environment.

On the East Coast, many New York department stores, including Gimbels, Bonwit Teller, Henri Bendel, Abraham & Straus, A.T. Stewart and B. Altman, shared a similar fate. In early 2019, Lord & Taylor sold its flagship store in Manhattan to WeWork, which offers shared workspaces, for $850 million. Fashion rental subscription service Le Tote, Inc., which is one-tenth the size of Lord & Taylor in terms of revenue, bought the chain for $74 million in August 2019. Le Tote envisions using Lord & Taylor's thirty-eight existing stores as rental pickup and return centers. Barney's, another luxury retailer, filed for bankruptcy in August 2019, citing rising rents and fewer customers.

Philadelphia had Strawbridge & Clothier and Wanamaker's, Chicago its beloved Marshall Field's, Minneapolis its Dayton's and Boston its Filene's.

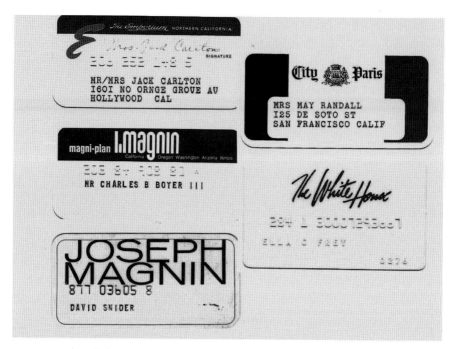

Loyal customers carried their proprietary store credit card; in those pre-chip days, the salesperson ran it through a swiper to take an impression. *Scott Nimmo.*

Sears, which once dominated the American retail landscape, filed for Chapter 11 bankruptcy protection in October 2018 but remains in business with a greatly reduced number of stores. One bright light is Nordstrom, which is still a retail force, perhaps because it invested heavily in e-commerce and was careful not to open too many stores. Despite those efforts, however, Nordstrom's share price is suffering; in August 2019, its stock price was down more than 50 percent from the highs of fall 2018.

San Francisco's retail scene continues to evolve. The old stores profiled in this book had a strong local presence and many years of success, but despite their many efforts to adapt and survive, they couldn't make it. What San Franciscans do have are the memories of a time full of characters and experiences, from riding the streetcar downtown to visit Santa at the Emporium to shopping for that "perfect something" at I. Magnin.

NOTES

Introduction

1. Frank Dunnigan, e-mail message to author, November 3, 2018.
2. "Ib," *Weekly Alta California* 1, no. 47, November 22, 1849, 1.
3. Issel and Cherny, *San Francisco*, 24.
4. Frank Pixely, "The Twenty 'Nice' Millionaires Who Live in San Francisco," *Argonaut* 13 (July 21, 1883): 9.
5. Irwin, *City that Was*, 28.
6. "Opening of the St. Francis," *San Francisco Chronicle*, March 22, 1904, 9.
7. Herb Caen, "More Than a Store," *San Francisco Chronicle*, December 5, 1994, C1.

Chapter 1

8. Jack Foisie, "Saga of a Shipload of Treasures," *San Francisco Chronicle*, April 30, 1950, 14.
9. *Brief History in Review of City of Paris.*
10. Soulé, *Annals of San Francisco*, 463.
11. Sylvia, *Sylvia's Book of the Toilet*, 89.
12. Altrocchi, *Spectacular San Franciscans*, 82.
13. Biétry-Salinger, "Histoire de la famille Verdier."
14. Ibid.

15. *Brief History in Review of City of Paris.*

16. Martha Hutson, "City of Paris: An Editorial," *American Art Review* 1, no. 5 (July 1974): 56–59.

17. *Why City of Paris Sells Wine*, pamphlet, n.d., San Francisco History Center, San Francisco Public Library.

18. "City of Paris Reaches 100ᵗʰ Year This Week," *San Francisco Examiner*, April 30, 1950.

19. Nora Boyd, "Life on Normandy Lane," *Examiner and Chronicle California Living Magazine*, June 17, 1979, 36.

20. "A Message," Paul L. Chauvin to the Many Good Customers, Friends and Business Associates of City of Paris and to All of Its Devoted Employees, January 25, 1972, San Francisco History Center, San Francisco Public Library.

21. Herb Caen, "The Walking Caen," *San Francisco Chronicle*, February 20, 1972, 113.

22. Paul Goldberger, "San Franciscans Get Three New Buildings," *New York Times*, November 15, 1983, 11.

Chapter 2

23. Dictation given in San Francisco by Raphael Weill, circa 1887–89, Box 4, Guide to the Miscellaneous California Dictations, Bancroft Library, Berkeley, California.

24. "Raphael Weill Resident Here 59 Years Friday," *San Francisco Call*, January 22, 1913, 1.

25. Maritime Heritage Project, "SS Brother Jonathan."

26. Neville, *Fantastic City*, 57.

27. James H. Wilkins, "Great Store Has Humble Beginning," *San Francisco Examiner*, May 9, 1930.

28. Atherton, *My San Francisco*, 50.

29. "White House Had 1ˢᵗ Page Advertisement," *San Francisco Call*, May 1, 1937.

30. Atherton, *My San Francisco*, 50.

31. "'San Francisco's First Citizen' Was Great City's Tribute to Raphael Weill," *Women's Wear Daily*, December 11, 1920, 44.

32. Wilkins, "Great Store."

33. "Spontaneous Ovations Greeted Raphael Weill, Veteran Merchant and Philanthropist, on His Return," *Women's Wear Daily*, July 19, 1919, 59.

34. Wilkins, "Great Store."

35. Harris, *Merchant Princes*, 240.

36. Dictation by Raphael Weill, Bancroft Library, Berkeley, California.

37. William M. Kramer and Norton Stern, "French Jews in the Early West: An Aristocratic Cousinhood," *Western States Jewish Historical Quarterly* 13 (July 1981): 322.

38. "Weill Quits S.F. Club as Nephew Is Barred as Member," *Los Angeles Herald*, October 23, 1914, 8.

39. Altrocchi, *Spectacular San Franciscans*, 288.

40. "White House Charms Throngs and Marks City's Recovery," *San Francisco Call*, March 14, 1909, 24.

41. "New White House Opens Under Brilliant Auspices," *San Francisco Chronicle*, March 14, 1909, 39.

42. "Great Business House: The Rise and Progress of the Leading Temple of Fashion on the Pacific Coast," *San Francisco Chronicle*, December 8, 1872, 5.

43. "Christmas Greeting: What to Buy and Where to Buy It," *San Francisco Chronicle*, December 17, 1882, 5.

44. "For Teen-Agers Only! Young Set Helps Design, Run New Clothes Shop," *San Francisco Examiner*, February 27, 1947.

45. "White House Teen Board," *San Francisco Examiner*, June 23, 1964.

46. Mildred Schroeder, "Frosting Finesse—A Fairy-Land Fantasy," *San Francisco Examiner*, March 6, 1961.

47. Roy Johns, "Focus: White House Post-Mortem," *Women's Wear Daily* 110, no. 21, February 1, 1965, 1, 26.

48. "Bedlam at White House—Bargains Draw Crowds," *San Francisco Examiner*, January 27, 1965, 16.

49. "White House Celebrates Founding Day," *San Francisco Examiner*, November 24, 1929.

Chapter 3

50. A.L. Gump and Frank J. Taylor, "Saloon to Salon," *Saturday Evening Post*, June 20, 1936, 70.

51. Esersky, et al., *Gump's since 1861*, 13.

52. Gump and Taylor, "Saloon to Salon," 74.

53. Gump, *Jade*, 221.

54. Post, *By Motor to the Golden Gate*, 221.

55. Wilson, *Gump's Treasure Trade*, 142.

56. Gump, et al., "Composer, Artist, and President of Gump's," 141.

57. Gump, *Good Taste Costs No More*.

58. Gump, et al., "Composer, Artist, and President of Gump's," 117.

59. Ibid., 208.

60. *San Francisco Chronicle*, September 25, 1988, 370.

61. Gump, et al., "Composer, Artist, and President of Gump's," 217.

62. "Richard Gump, Longtime Boss of Famed S.F. Store," *San Francisco Chronicle*, September 6, 1989, 24.

63. Gump, et al., "Composer, Artist, and President of Gump's," 256.

64. Ibid., 238.

65. Sophia Kunthara, "Famed SF Retail Store Gump's Is Coming Back. It May Just Not Be in San Francisco," *San Francisco Chronicle*, June 29, 2019.

Chapter 4

66. Joan Juliet Buck, "How a Great Store Stays Personal," *Vogue*, September 1976, 356.

67. "Matriarch Magnin," *Time*, no. 7, February 17, 1936.

68. Magnin, "Call Me Mr. Grover," 2.

69. Ibid., 3.

70. Buck, "How a Great Store Stays Personal," 376.

71. Magnin and Robins, *Call Me Cyril*, 14.

72. "Matriarch Magnin."

73. "Magnins Open Magnificent New Home at Grant Avenue and Geary Street," *San Francisco Chronicle*, May 9, 1909, 33.

74. Magnin, "Call Me Mr. Grover," 2.

75. David Colen, "The Store that Made California Fashionable," *Town and Country* 129 (August 1976), 49.

76. Joseph, "Reminiscences," 5.

77. Magnin, "Call Me Mr. Grover," 11.

78. Ibid., 9.

79. "Bullock's and I. Magnin & Co. Plan Merger," *Los Angeles Times*, February 3, 1944, 1.

80. "Brief History of I. Magnin & Company," undated, c. 1942, I. Magnin Records, Company History files, San Francisco History Center, San Francisco Public Library.

81. Herb Caen, "The Walking Caen," *San Francisco Chronicle*, August 14, 1966, 86.

82. Herb Caen, "More Than a Store," *San Francisco Chronicle*, December 5, 1994, C1.

83. Pat Steger, "After 118 Years, I. Magnin Takes a Powder," *San Francisco Chronicle*, January 7, 1995, A1.

84. Los Angeles and San Francisco Bureaus, "The Two Magnins," *Women's Wear Daily*, November 3, 1967, 4–5.

85. Jon Greer, "Why Macy's Wants I. Magnin," *San Francisco Chronicle*, April 6, 1988, C1.

86. Caen, "More Than a Store."

Chapter 5

87. Marilyn Lewis, "Baghdad by the Bay San Francisco," Facebook group, www.facebook.com/groups/1435627060034188/search/?query=marilyn%20lewis&epa=SEARCH_BOX.

88. Jack London, "South of the Slot," *Saturday Evening Post*, May 22, 1909, 3.

89. Jack McLaughlin, "We Grew Up In San Francisco," Facebook group, www.facebook.com/groups/sanfrancisconative/search/?query=mcLaughlin%20emporium&epa=SEARCH_BOX.

90. "We Grew Up in San Francisco," Facebook group, www.facebook.com/groups/sanfrancisconative.

91. Ibid.

92. Peter Hartlaub, "Emporium's Santa Was a Rock Star," *San Francisco Chronicle*, December 17, 2012, 34.

93. "We Grew Up in San Francisco," Facebook group.

94. Gavin Power and Kenneth Howe, "Shoppers Mourn End of Emporium Era," *San Francisco Chronicle*, August 16, 1995, 1.

95. *Bay of San Francisco*.

96. Terry, "Frederick William Dohrmann."

97. Dohrmann, "History of the Preliminaries."

98. "The Finest Store in All the World," *San Francisco Chronicle*, May 23, 1896, 9.

99. Terry, "Frederick William Dohrmann."

100. Dohrmann, "History of the Preliminaries."

101. "Emporium Management Entertains Employees," *San Francisco Call*, October 18, 1899, 14.

102. "Earthquake and Fire: San Francisco in Ruins," *Call-Chronicle-Examiner*, April 19, 1906, 1.

103. Cosgrove and Cosgrove, *California Potpourri*.

104. "The Emporium Spreading Out," *San Francisco Chronicle*, July 29, 1906, 26.

105. "Emporium to Celebrate 20 Years' Success," *San Francisco Chronicle*, May 21, 1916, 29.

106. "The Emporium Has Reopened," *San Francisco Chronicle*, October 2, 1908, 7.

107. Dohrmann, "Convention of Affiliated Stores."

Chapter 6

108. Joseph Magnin, "Joseph Magnin Wants You," advertisement, catalogue, November 12, 1971.

109. MacKenzie, *BRUMAC Study*.

110. Magnin and Robins, *Call Me Cyril*, 9.

111. Ibid.

112. Cynthia Robins, "The Magnin Legacy," *San Francisco Chronicle*, February 19, 1989, 18.

113. Ibid., 29.

114. Samuel Feinberg, "Joseph Magnin's Reins Held by Third Generations," *Women's Wear Daily*, July 3, 1968, 8.

115. Suzanne Harris, "How Corporate Gray Collided with the Flash and Dash at Joseph Magnin," *Los Angeles Times*, December 5, 1982, 8

116. Cynthia Robins and Burr Snider, "Why J. Magnin's Ran Down," *San Francisco Examiner*, September 18, 1984, C1.

BIBLIOGRAPHY

Books

Altrocchi, Julia Cooley. *The Spectacular San Franciscans*. New York: E.P. Dutton and Company, Inc., 1949.

Atherton, G.F. *My San Francisco: A Wayward Biography*. Indianapolis: Bobbs-Merrill Company, 1946.

Barth, Gunther. *City People: The Rise of Modern City Culture in Nineteenth-Century America.* New York: Oxford University Press on Demand, 1982.

The Bay of San Francisco: The Metropolis of the Pacific Coast, and Its Suburban Cities: A History. Chicago: Lewis Publishing Company, 1892.

Benson, Susan Porter. *Counter Cultures: Saleswomen, Managers, and Customers in American Department Stores, 1890–1940*. Urbana: University of Illinois Press, 1988.

Biétry-Salinger, Jehanne. "Histoire de la famille Verdier." In *Guide Franco-Californien du Centenaire*. San Francisco: Pisani Print and Publishing Company, 1949.

Birmingham, Nan Tillson. *Store.* New York: Putnam, 1978.

Birmingham, Stephen. *The Right People*. Boston: Little, Brown and Co., 1968.

Bronner, Simon J. *Consuming Visions: Accumulation and Display of Goods in America, 1880–1920*. New York: Norton, 1989.

Chalmers, Claudine. *French San Francisco*. Charleston, SC: Arcadia Publishing, 2007.

Cosgrove, Carole Jane, and Emilie Dohrmann Cosgrove, eds. *California Potpourri, 1852–1936*. Los Angeles: Jeffries Banknote, 1966.

Decker, Peter R. *Fortunes and Failures: White-Collar Mobility in Nineteenth-Century San Francisco*. Cambridge, MA: Harvard University Press, 1978.

Donovan, Frances R. *The Saleslady*. Chicago: University of Chicago Press, 1929.

Eisenberg, Ellen, Ava Kahn and William Toll. *Jews of the Pacific Coast: Reinventing Community on America's Edge*. Seattle: University of Washington Press, 2010.

Esersky, Gareth Lauren, et. al. *Gump's since 1861: A San Francisco Legend*. San Francisco: Chronicle Books, 1991.

Frick, Devin T. *I. Magnin & Co.: A California Legacy*. Orange County, CA: Park Place Press, 2000.

Fussell, Paul. *Class: A Guide Through the American Status System*. New York: Simon & Schuster, 1992.

Gump, Richard. *Good Taste Costs No More*. New York: Doubleday, 1951.

———. *Jade: Stone of Heaven*. New York: Doubleday, 1962.

Harris, Leon A. *Merchant Princes: An Intimate History of Jewish Families Who Built Great Department Stores*. New York: Berkley Books, 1980.

Hendrickson, Robert. *The Grand Emporiums: The Illustrated History of America's Great Department Stores*. New York: Stein and Day, 1980.

Holbrook, Stewart Hall. *The Age of the Moguls: Stewart H. Holbrook*. Garden City, NY: Doubleday, 1953.

Howard, Vicki. *From Main Street to Mall: The Rise and Fall of the American Department Store*. Philadelphia: University of Pennsylvania Press, 2015.

Irwin, Will. *The City that Was: A Requiem of Old San Francisco*. New York: B.W. Huebsch, 1908.

Isenberg, Alison. *Designing San Francisco: Art, Land, and Urban Renewal in the City by the Bay*. Princeton, NJ: Princeton University Press, 2017.

Issel, William, and Robert W. Cherny. *San Francisco, 1865–1932: Politics, Power, and Urban Development*. Berkeley: University of California Press, 1986.

Kahn, Judd. *Imperial San Francisco: Politics and Planning in an American City, 1897–1906*. Lincoln: University of Nebraska Press, 1979.

Levy, Harriet Lane. *920 O'Farrell Street: A Jewish Girlhood in Old San Francisco*. Berkeley, CA: Heyday Press, 1996.

Lewis, Oscar. *This Was San Francisco: Being First-hand Accounts of the Evolution of One of America's Favorite Cities*. New York: D. McKay, 1962.

Linsteadt, Sylvia. *Lost Worlds of the San Francisco Bay Area*. Berkeley, CA: Heyday, 2017.

Longstreth, Richard W. *The American Department Store Transformed, 1920–1960.* New Haven, CT: Yale University Press, 2010.

Lotchin, Roger W. *San Francisco, 1846–1856.* Urbana: University of Illinois Press, 1997.

MacKenzie, Murray L. *The BRUMAC Study: A Report to Joseph Magnin Company on Its Image and Shopping Patterns in the Berkeley Market.* Berkeley: University of California Press, 1965.

Maclean, Annie Marion. *Women Workers and Society.* Chicago: A.C. McClurg, 1916.

Magnin, Cyril, and Cynthia Robins. *Call Me Cyril.* New York: McGraw-Hill, 1981.

Mahoney, Tom, and Leonard Sloane. *The Great Merchants: America's Foremost Retail Institutions and the People Who Made Them Great.* New York: Harper & Row, 1974.

Marcus, Leonard S. *The American Store Window.* New York: Whitney Library of Design, 1978.

Meyer, Karl E., and Shareen Blair Brysac. *The China Collectors: America's Century-Long Hunt for Asian Art Treasures.* New York: Palgrave Macmillan, 2015.

Mullane, James Thomas. *A Store to Remember.* San Ramon, CA: Falcon Books, 2007.

Muscatine, Doris. *Old San Francisco: The Biography of a City from Early Days to the Earthquake.* New York: G.P. Putnam, 1975.

Neville, Amelia Ransome. *The Fantastic City.* New York: Arno Press, 1975, ca 1932.

Poletti, Therese. *Art Deco San Francisco: The Architecture of Timothy Pflueger.* New York: Princeton Architectural Press, 2008.

Post, Emily. *By Motor to the Golden Gate.* New York: D. Appleton & Co., 1916.

Rosenbaum, Fred. *Cosmopolitans: A Social and Cultural History of the Jews of the San Francisco Bay Area.* Berkeley: University of California Press, 2009.

Sewell, Jessica Ellen. *Women and the Everyday City: Public Space in San Francisco, 1890–1915.* Minneapolis: University of Minnesota Press, 2011.

Siefkin, David. *Meet Me at the St. Francis: The First Seventy-Five Years of a Great San Francisco Hotel.* San Francisco: St. Francis Hotel Corp., ca 1979.

Soulé, Frank, ed. *Annals of San Francisco.* New York: D. Appleton & Co., 1854.

Starr, Kevin. *Golden Dreams: California in an Age of Abundance, 1950–1963.* New York: Oxford University Press, 2011.

Sylvia. *Sylvia's Book of the Toilet: A Ladies Guide to Dress and Beauty.* London: Ward, Lock, & Co., 1881.

Underhill, Paco. *The Call of the Mall: How We Shop*. London: Profile, 2005.
———. *What Women Want: The Global Market Turns Female-Friendly*. New York: Simon & Schuster, 2011.
———. *Why We Buy: The Science of Shopping*. New York: Simon & Schuster Paperbacks, 2009.
Veblen, Thorstein. *Conspicuous Consumption*. New York: Penguin Books, 2006.
———. *The Theory of the Leisure Class*. New York: Macmillan, 1899.
Warren, William. *Merchant of Sonoma: Chuck Williams, Pioneer of the American Kitchen*. San Francisco: Weldon Owen, 2011.
Whitaker, Jan. *Service and Style*. New York: St. Martin's Press, 2007.
———. *A World of Department Stores*. New York: Vendome Press, 2011.
Wilson, Carol Green. *Gump's Treasure Trade: A Story of San Francisco*. New York: Crowell, 1965.
Yarrow, Kit. *Decoding the New Consumer Mind: How and Why We Shop and Buy*. San Francisco: Jossey-Bass, 2014.

Newspapers

Argonaut
Daily Alta California
Los Angeles Herald
Los Angeles Times
New York Times
San Francisco Call
San Francisco Chronicle
San Francisco Examiner
Women's Wear Daily

Magazines

American Art Review
California Living Magazine
Moment
Saturday Evening Post
Time
Town and Country
Vogue

Journals

Western States Jewish Historical Quarterly

Websites

Bravo, Tony. "Favorite SF Powder Room? Women Remember I. Magnin's Marble Oasis at Macy's." *San Francisco Chronicle*, February 4, 2019. www.sfchronicle.com/style/article/Favorite-SF-powder-room-Women-remember-I-13581742.php#photo-16861994.

Gillick, Jeremy. "Jews and the San Francisco Gold Rush." *Moment*, May 20, 2013. www.momentmag.com/jews-and-the-san-francisco-gold-rush-2.

Hartlaub, Peter. "Remembering the City of Paris Department Store (Photos)." SF Gate, October 6, 2011. blog.sfgate.com/thebigevent/2011/10/06/remembering-the-city-of-paris-department-store-photos.

Jewish Museum of the American West. "Early Pioneer French Jews of California." June 18, 2014. www.jmaw.org/french-jews-california-pioneer.

———. "Isaac & Mary Ann Cohen Magnin: Early Jewish Pioneer Fashion Leaders of California." June 30, 2015. www.jmaw.org/magnin-jewish-san-francisco.

Kamiya, Gary. "SF's Early German Jews Quickly Became an Aristocracy." *San Francisco Chronicle*, September 2, 2017. www.sfchronicle.com/bayarea/article/Early-SF-s-German-Jews-quickly-became-an-12168096.php.

Leishman, Nora. "The City of Paris: Historical Essay." Shaping San Francisco's Digital Archive @ FoundSF. www.foundsf.org/index.php?title=The_City_of_Paris.

Ma, Annie. "Macy's to Sell Former I. Magnin Building at Union Square." SF Gate, February 27, 2018. www.sfgate.com/bayarea/article/Macy-s-to-sell-former-I-Magnin-building-at-12711124.php.

The Maritime Heritage Project. "Raphael Weill." www.maritimeheritage.org/vips/Raphael-Weill.html.

———. "SS Brother Jonathan." www.maritimeheritage.org/passengers/Brother-Jonathan-18June1854.html.

NoeHill in San Francisco. "City of Paris Building." noehill.com/sf/landmarks/nat1975000471.asp.

Nuno, Gregory J. "A History of Union Square." *The Argonaut* 4, no. 1 (Summer 1993). www.foundsf.org/index.php?title=A_HISTORY_OF_UNION_SQUARE.

Steger, Pat. "A Fitting Tribute / Joseph Magnin Employees Gather to Remember the Store with a Style All Its Own." SF Gate, April 6, 1999. www.sfgate.com/entertainment/article/A-Fitting-Tribute-Joseph-Magnin-employees-2938077.php.

Terry, Carole. "Frederick William Dohrmann (1842–1914)." Immigrant Entrepreneurship: German-American Business Biographies, 1720 to the Present. June 16, 2015. www.immigrantentrepreneurship.org/entry.php?rec=241#.ViLLGS5CtJg.mailto.

Other Material

Brief History in Review of City of Paris, San Francisco's Oldest and Most Interesting Store. Pamphlet. n.d. California Historical Society Archives, San Francisco, California.

Dorhmann, F.W. "Convention of Affiliated Stores." Minutes, Opening Address, September 27, 1913. Author's collection.

———. "History of the Preliminaries of the Formation of the Emporium and Golden Rule Bazaar." Report, 1897.

Gump, Richard Benjamin, Suzanne B. Riess, Johanna Sianta, Ken Kojima, Paul Faria and Clariece Graham. "Composer, Artist, and President of Gump's, San Francisco: Oral History Transcript." Berkeley: University of California, 1989.

Joseph, Edwin, V.P. of Stores. "Reminiscences." Unpublished memoir, 1959. I. Magnin Records, Company History files, San Francisco History Center, San Francisco Public Library, 5.

Magnin, Grover. "Call Me Mr. Grover." Unpublished memoir. I. Magnin Records, Company History files, San Francisco History Center, San Francisco Public Library.

Page and Turnbull. "The Former White House Department Store, San Francisco, CA: Existing & Historic Building Conditions Report for a Proposed Major Expansion of the Banana Republic Store." San Francisco, California: Page & Turnbull, 1966.

Weill, Raphael. Dictation given in San Francisco, ca. 1887–89. Box 4, Guide to the Miscellaneous California Dictations, Bancroft Library, Berkeley, California.

INDEX

ABOUT THE AUTHOR

Anne Evers Hitz is a fifth-generation San Franciscan and a great-great-granddaughter of one of the Emporium department store's founders, F.W. Dohrmann. She is the author of *Emporium Department Store* (Arcadia Publishing, 2014) and *San Francisco's Ferry Building* (Arcadia Publishing, 2017).

A graduate of UC Berkeley, Hitz is a writer, editor and project manager who has had her own communications consulting firm in San Francisco for over twenty-five years. She also worked as publicity director for the University of California Press and as an editorial assistant at publishers Oxford University Press and Farrar, Straus & Giroux in New York.

Hitz has had a long interest in San Francisco history, its lore and legends. She is a guide for City Guides, a group of local volunteers who give free walking tours of San Francisco.

Hitz hopes that this cultural history of the old stores of San Francisco will bring back fond memories and inspire the telling of more colorful stories.